PACIFIC RIM NATIONAL PARK

Fisheries Restoration Interpretive Drive

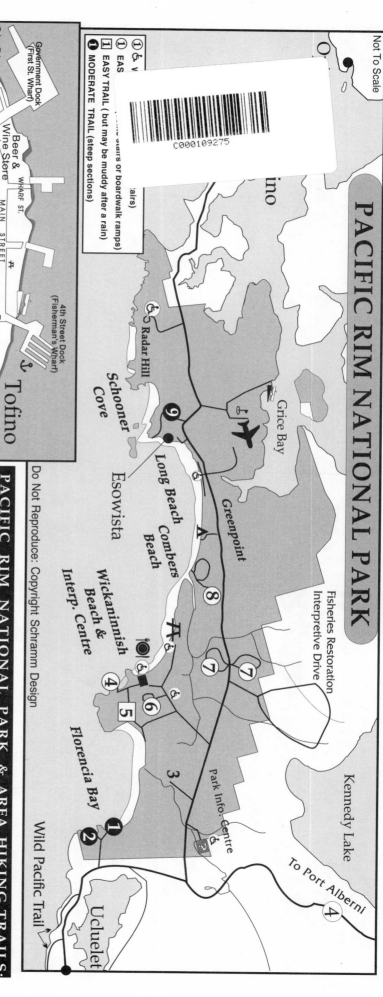

Legend:
- ① & v...
- ① EAS...
- ① EASY TRAIL (but may be muddy after a rain)
- ① MODERATE TRAIL (steep sections)
- ...stairs or boardwalk ramps)

Map labels: Tofino, Radar Hill, Schooner Cove, Long Beach, Combers Beach, Esowista, Wickaninnish Beach & Interp. Centre, Greenpoint, Grice Bay, Florencia Bay, Wild Pacific Trail, Park Info. Centre, Ucluelet, Kennedy Lake, To Port Alberni

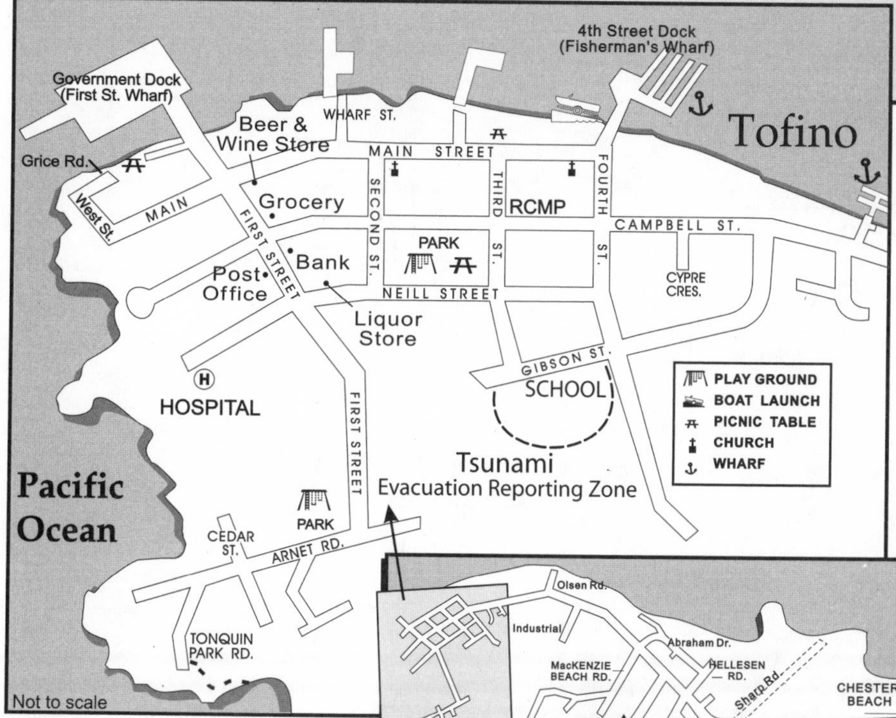

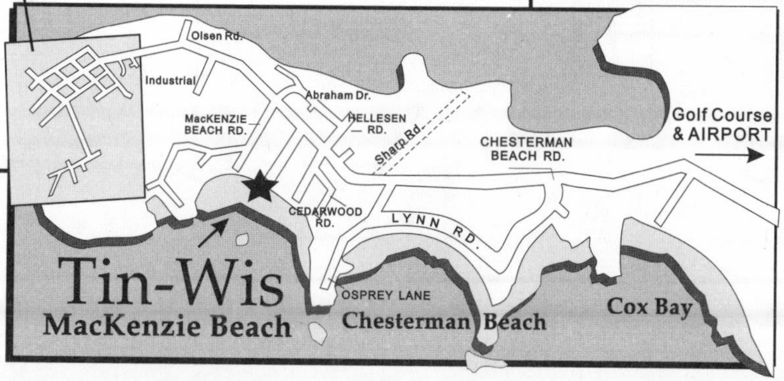

PACIFIC RIM NATIONAL PARK & AREA HIKING TRAILS:

1 & 2. **Willowbrae:** 3.4 km wooded trail to scenic Halfmoon Bay or Florencia Beach. **Steep.**

3. **Gold Mine:** This trail is **CLOSED** due to wave errosion near the beach. No access.

4. **South Beach:** 1.5 km - along scenic beach to a musical pebble beach. **Steep ramp & stairs.**

5. **Nuu-chah-nulth:** 2.5 km First Nations Interpretive trail connects Long Beach to Florencia. **Steep ramp & stairs.**

6. **Bog Trail:** .8 km boardwalk loop interprets ancient stunted trees & deep moss. No stairs.

7. **Rainforest:** Two 1km loops explores ancient rainforests. Interpretive signs. Few stairs.

8. **Spruce Fringe:** 1.5 km loop interprets giant trees & wind effects. Short stairs & boardwalk.

9. **Schooner:** 1 km mossy forest trail from a stream gorge to a secluded beach. Steep trail.

Wild Pacific Trail: cliff-side trail. Easy, 2.7 km at lighthouse; or 4 km near Willowbrae Trail.

Wickaninnish Interpretive Centre: Large displays and programs in Pacific Rim Park.

Raincoast Interp. Centre: interesting displays and programs in Tofino.

SAFETY INFORMATION:

Waves & Rip Currents: Ocean is dangerous and cold year round.

Living with Wildlife: NEVER feed animals, keep food locked up, when driving pull over to view wildlife, do not collect natural objects or plants.

If you face a cougar or bear: Pick up small children, do not run, face animal and retreat slowly. IF attacked be aggressive, do not play dead.

Leash Dogs: Dogs MUST be on a lease on any trail or beach in the area. Pick up more safety information from Parks Information Centres.

Tofino (town map)

Government Dock (First St. Wharf), Grice Rd., West St., MAIN ST., WHARF ST., Beer & Wine Store, Grocery, Post Office, Bank, HOSPITAL, CEDAR ST., ARNET RD., TONQUIN PARK RD., PARK, Liquor Store, FIRST STREET, SECOND ST., NEILL STREET, THIRD ST., GIBSON ST., SCHOOL, Tsunami Evacuation Reporting Zone, RCMP, FOURTH ST., CAMPBELL ST., CYPRE CRES., 4th Street Dock (Fisherman's Wharf)

Legend: PLAY GROUND · BOAT LAUNCH · PICNIC TABLE · CHURCH · WHARF

Pacific Ocean

Not to scale

Tin-Wis

MacKenzie Beach, Industrial, Olsen Rd., MacKENZIE BEACH RD., Abraham Dr., MELLESEN, Sharp Rd., CEDARWOOD RD., LYNN RD., OSPREY LANE, CHESTERMAN BEACH RD., Chesterman Beach, Cox Bay, Golf Course & AIRPORT

Not to scale

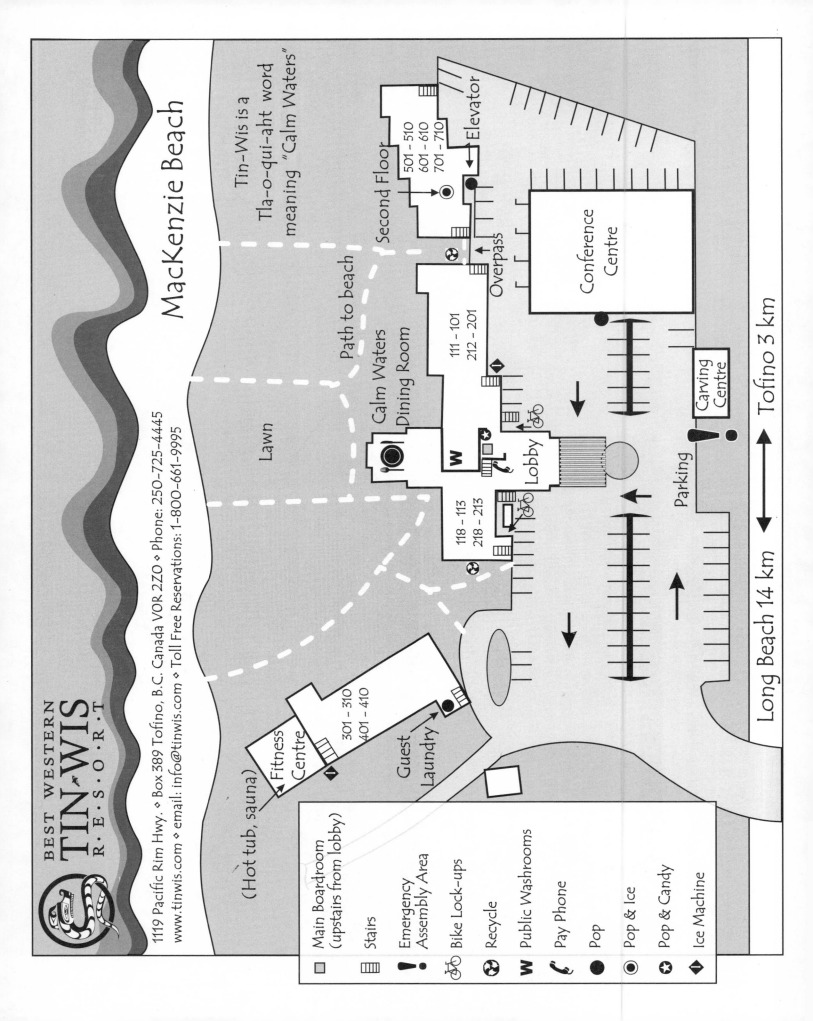

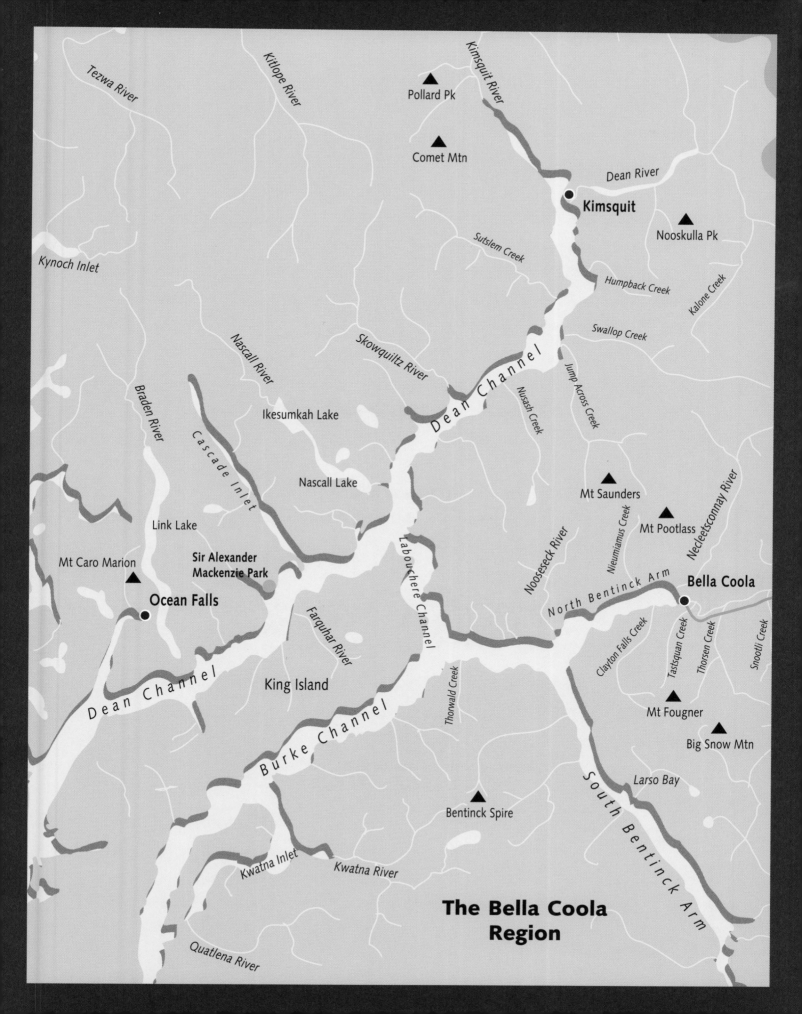

The Bella Coola Region

Michael Weigl

Hans Gummmmmler

Thanks

to our sponsors

West Coast Helicopters Maintenance & Contracting Ltd.
OVER 18 YEARS & 18,000+ HOURS SAFE FLYING
OF THE NORTH ISLAND & MIDCOAST

Bella Coola

Bella Coola

Life in the Heart
of the Coast Mountains

Hans Granander and Michael Wigle

HARBOUR PUBLISHING

CONTENTS

Foreword
by Leslie Kopas

Occasionally, someone fascinated by my peculiarities will ask, "Where are you from?"

"Bella Coola," I reply.

"You know," they say, "I've been intending for a long time to see that place. I hear it's beautiful country."

"It is," I confirm proudly, as though I had something to do with it. The talk moves on to where Bella Coola is exactly, to the Native Indians, to what people do, to grizzly bears, to the Hill. You can talk for a long time about Bella Coola.

From the outside, the entire Bella Coola valley is called Bella Coola; the name even annexes the Atnarko valley. In the valley you get specific: the Townsite, the Village, Four Mile, Lower Bella Coola, Hagensborg, Salloomt, Nusatsum, Canoe Crossing, Firvale, Stuie, Atnarko. Each place is drier than the last. That's because the Bella Coola valley cuts through the Coast Mountains from the Pacific Ocean to the Interior Plateau. Each place has its own personality and culture. The Townsite is town; the Village and Four Mile are Nuxalk Indian; Lower Bella Coola, Hagensborg and

Page 1:
Skier above South
Bentinck Arm.

Page 2-3:
Sunset over Cultus
Sound, near Hunter
Island.

Page 4-5:
Grizzly bear on Atnarko
River.

Page 6-7:
Mt. Nusatsum.

Above:
Welcome to Bella Coola.

Right:
A bull rider at the Bella
Coola rodeo.

Opposite:
Bella Coola townsite
tucked in amongst the
towering Coast Mountains.
The silty river feeds one
of the largest estuaries
on the Central Coast.

Above:
Check your brakes.

Below:
Aerial view of the lower
Bella Coola valley facing
west to the ocean.

Opposite:
Orbital Spire along the
crest of the Nusatsum
and Cacoohtin valleys.

Salloomt evolved from Norwegian farms; Firvale has the feel of the Interior, the edge of dry country; Stuie is the lodge and Tweedsmuir Park; Atnarko is the edge of wilderness and the bottom of the Hill. The Hill is Bella Coola's most famous personality, the first one encountered on entering the valley, the last one on the way out—and not forgotten. Everyone talks about the Hill; guidebook writers love it.

The names and their location are part of local knowledge. Being only three blocks long, even the Townsite is not readily apparent to an outsider. Several years ago a teacher and her family drove into the valley keeping a close eye out for Bella Coola or a population centre worthy of a school. When they were halted by the brow log on the wharf at the waterfront, they knew they had seen the entire Bella Coola valley, but had somehow missed Bella Coola. Topography dominates the place, dwarfing human works. This can be disconcerting to urban people.

Newcomers observe the differences in the natural world as they travel through the valley before they sense the differences in the human communities. After the descent of the Hill, the flat of the Atnarko valley is a balm, the big Douglas fir trees acting like cathedral walls—a cathedral in which grizzlies live. Big mountains rear up; the first is Stupendous Mountain, which Alexander Mackenzie named two centuries ago. In the middle of the valley—the middle of the Coast Mountains—the peaks poke spires into the sky. In the lower valley they lose their exuberance a little.

In autumn, snow descends the mountains in measured steps, drawing precise contour

lines at freezing level: white above, dark below. A warm westerly blows in, erasing the most recent line, and melted snow comes down in a rage. Eventually the snow wins out until spring. In summer, once in a while, thunderstorms provide a show: lightning flashes, thunder echoes off valley walls, halfway up a mountain a struck tree flares up, clouds dump water on it. Briefly the world is full of energy, then returns to the long patience of the mountains.

In autumn, as the snow descends, so does the sun. It eventually skims the tops of the mountains, and then appears only briefly through side valley gaps. From time to time the Interior Plateau sends down its winter climate carried on a frigid east wind, using the Bella Coola as a funnel to the Pacific Ocean. The sun does not reach the valley bottom, but the mountains sparkle. They are most beautiful when the weather is bitter. In February the sun climbs above the tops of the mountains again and there is joy in the valley.

The sun draws eulachons to the Bella Coola River. Mew gulls are ecstatic, the eagles interested but dignified. Otters patrol the river in processions, diving and rising like little Ogopogos. Trumpeter swans fly past on their way to the tide flats, sounding like a children's band with bad instruments under a bad conductor. Ravens talk to each other in Sitka spruce thickets, keeping in touch: "Hello, Milo." "Hello, Donald."

In summer the high country clears its snow for meadows of flowers. Caribou, always on the move, skittery about wolves, move in to join marmots and ptarmigan. Moose feed where meadow meets forest. Mountain goats feed where meadow meets

The Robson homestead on the upper Atnarko River, a major tributary of the Bella Coola.

alpine tundra. There are lots of mosquitoes—lots and lots.

The first European to travel through the Bella Coola valley was Alexander Mackenzie. He published a book about it in 1801—an excellent report, but with no pictures.

A photographic record of Bella Coola began in June 1873, when the Commissioner of Indian Affairs arrived for a day accompanied by Richard Maynard, a photographer. They took several photographs of the Nuxalk village near the mouth of the Bella Coola River. Exactly eight years later the Commissioner returned with another photographer, Edward Dossetter. They photographed the village again.

In 1885 B.F. Jacobsen, a Norwegian collector for European museums, took nine Nuxalk men to Germany for a year to exhibit Nuxalk culture, particularly masked dances. A German photographer, Carl Gunther, took many photographs of them. The Nuxalk name for Jacobsen was *Klolkva*, which means "he who takes or buys everything he sees."

Early in 1896 Simon Bangen, a professional photographer, joined Norwegian settlers in Bella Coola. He returned to Minnesota in July 1897. He did not like Bella Coola. Not everyone did.

Iver Fougner, who came with the first bunch of Norwegians in October 1894, admitted right away: "I feel like leaving the valley, but as I have no place to go I may as well stay here." He stayed for the rest of his life and took excellent photographs of both the Nuxalk and Norwegian settlements. On a visit to Norway, he showed his photographs to a young ethnologist named Thor Heyerdahl, who saw great similarities

Heritage house in Hagensborg, built in 1914.

between the appearance of the Nuxalkmc and their art and those of the Polynesians he knew. Heyerdahl came to Bella Coola to see for himself and developed original ideas about human migration by sea. The *Kon-Tiki* expedition was his first practical test.

While Fougner was still taking photographs, Harlan Smith, an ethnographer working for the National Museum of Canada, arrived. He wanted to capture Bella Coola on film. Between 1920 and 1924 he took more than a thousand photographs. He should have received the Nuxalk name Klolkva; he took everything he saw.

In October 1933 Clifford Kopas, another candidate for the name Klolkva, rode a horse into Bella Coola from Alberta. He stayed to take more than a thousand black-and-white photographs over the next 20 years before he switched to colour. He was much more an artist than Harlan Smith; he wanted not only to show Bella Coola, but to show it beautifully. He also wrote many articles about the Central Coast.

Hans Granander and Mike Wigle have continued, albeit with different emphasis, what Cliff Kopas set out to do. The advance of scientific knowledge and of photographic technology have provided a deeper understanding of Bella Coola and the means to display its beauty more fully in pictures. Without long lenses, Cliff Kopas

Kayaking on the outer coast is quickly growing in popularity. The Discovery Coast ferry accommodates 'wet launches' and local guiding operations are springing up in Klemtu and Bella Bella.

did not attempt portraits of grizzly bears, for example, which Mike Wigle has done so successfully. Moreover, colour photography has been perfected in the intervening years—not to mention book publishing—and history has continued to unfold.

When I was a youngster, Bella Coola was not a special place to me. It just was. I knew no other place. There was no way out except by Union Steamship, if you could afford the fare and time. Outsider visitors were few. Since then I have seen quite a bit of the world, and have found most places interesting. But Bella Coola really is special because of its tremendous variety. It is a place for people who pay attention, who look closely. The beauty of the mountains is apparent to everyone. It takes the mind and spirit of an artist, a scientist and an explorer to look deeply into the beauty and variety of Bella Coola. Hans Granander and Mike Wigle have returned from their quest to show us what they have found.

—Leslie Kopas, July 2003

Note: *Leslie Kopas is the author of* Bella Coola Country *(Illahee Publishing, 2003), an annotated collection of photographs taken by his father, Bella Coola pioneer Cliff Kopas.*

Two eagles locked in competition for a seal carcass washed ashore on the Bella Coola tidal flats.

Introduction

In his foreword, Leslie Kopas makes an interesting point about the different things people mean when they say "Bella Coola." Locals tend to mean only "town," the compact grid of streets near the south side of the Bella Coola River mouth where the densest concentration of both First Nations and non-Native people live today. Outsiders tend to mean the whole 60-kilometre (40-mile) long Bella Coola valley. Bella Coola has yet a third level of meaning that it is important to recognize, since it is one the authors often use in this book.

Increasingly Bella Coola has come to be identified not just with the town, the river, the valley and the people, but with the whole surrounding region of mountainous wilderness and sparsely inhabited coastal inlets where Bella Coola is the largest and best-known centre. People sometimes give notice of this usage by attaching the words "area" or "country," as in: "Before I get too old, I'd love to go up and see that Bella Coola country." This regional sense of Bella Coola may include such far-flung points as Oweekeno, Bella Bella, Namu, Ocean Falls, Kimsquit, Lonesome Lake and Tweedsmuir Park, and may even extend into the provincial Interior as far as Anahim Lake—completely autonomous communities, some of them as far apart by normally travelled routes as London is from Edinburgh, but compressed into one neighbourhood by a wilderness whose vastness makes miles seem small. People in official government circles encourage this unified view by bundling the territory together in huge administrative jurisdictions centred on Bella Coola. The civil authority for the area is the Central Coast Regional District (CCRD), which embraces 2.7 million hectares (6.7 million acres) and is headquartered at Bella Coola. With a population of only 4,000 and a roomy 675 hectares (1,668 acres) for each resident, the CCRD has one of the lowest population densities of any habitable area on earth. It is one of the few large regions in North America where Native people outnumber non-Natives, and bears outnumber both.

The Bella Coola district has long been synonymous in the popular mind with "darkest British Columbia," but its reputation as the last stand of North America's great western wilderness took a quantum leap during the 1990s when the international environmental movement made it the target of an aggressive rainforest protection campaign. Christening the area with the *nom de guerre* "Great Bear Rainforest," a coalition of global and BC-based groups including Greenpeace, the Sierra Club, the Natural Resources Defence Council and the Raincoast Conservation Society began pumping out news stories, books, TV specials and films proselytizing the area as "a remote, rugged expanse of misty islands and fjords ... one of the last relatively undisturbed precincts left of the swath of giant trees, wild salmon runs, and abundant wildlife that once stretched from mid-California to southern Alaska." As envisioned by its advocates, this newly christened ecological province extended to Alaska in the north and Knight Inlet in the south, but it focussed strongly on the Central Coast:

Opposite:
A small rainforest stream near Hagensborg in the Bella Coola valley.

Below:
Ruffed grouse.

the charismatic kermode bear of Princess Royal Island became the poster child of the campaign, and the most heated demonstrations took place just next door to Bella Coola on King Island. Celebrities like Oprah Winfrey and Robert Kennedy Jr. lent their names to the cause, and by the end of the century the coalition had succeeded in placing Bella Coola country beside the endangered rain forests of Brazil and Indonesia as an internationally recognized environmental hot spot.

The environmental campaign had two important results. First, it raised the profile of the Central Coast as one of the earth's great surviving wilderness areas. Second, on April 4, 2001, the government entered into a protocol agreement with First Nations, forest companies and environmental groups to give the Central Coast a new million-plus-hectare conservation area. As Ujjal Dosanjh, then premier of BC, said in making the announcement, "The area referred to as the Great Bear Rainforest is an icon of the unique environmental and cultural values BC can share with the world. All of the people involved in this decision—First Nations, environmentalists, industry, workers, communities and government—have recognized what's at stake, and have fulfilled BC's role as an environmental leader on the world stage." Added to its already impressive roster of protected areas, which includes the Fjordland Recreation Area

Nascall River looking towards Ikesumkah Lake is a prime example of the scenic jewels waiting to be discovered in the Coast Mountains.

(84,000 hectares), the Kitlope Conservancy (321,000 hectares), the Hakai Conservation Area (123,000 hectares) and Tweedsmuir Provincial Park (981,000 hectares), the new preserve gave the Central Coast one of the largest and most diverse aggregations of protected wilderness in Canada, creating a veritable west coast Serengeti with grizzlies and mountain goats in place of elephants and lions. The agreement set in motion an intensive round of planning aimed at establishing appropriate management for the new wilderness areas, giving First Nations a stronger voice and exploring the conservation economy to augment traditional resource extraction.

Although worldwide awareness of the Bella Coola region's great natural attributes rose to an all-time high during this period, people who knew the area, the authors among them, had been attentive to its awesome wilderness values for years. When they speak of life in the heart of the Coast Mountains, they refer not just to the communities, indigenous peoples and fascinating human history of the area. Equally important, they mean to evoke the natural history of the rivers, the forests, the wildlife and the very mountains of the Bella Coola region, and their love and knowledge of those subjects fills the pages that follow.

—The Editors

Floodplain rain forest.

CHAPTER 1

A Magnificent Landscape

Previous pages:
Mt. Nusatsum, the
mountain that presides
over the Bella Coola
world.

Above:
Windswept outcrop, outer
coast.

Below:
Aerial view of glacier-
sculpted mountains,
Kitimat Range.

The Central Coast has a number of distinctly different landscape types and ecological zones. The outer coast, known as the Hecate Lowlands Ecosection, is an archipelago of low-lying rocky islands covered with scrubby forests and muskeg. This extremely intricate coastline of almost deserted bays, lagoons and kelp beds is a pleasure boater's adventure, though a challenging one.

Moving inland, the Coast Mountains appear to erupt from the sea, reaching up to permanently snow-capped heights of more than 2,250 metres (7,400 feet). Evergreen forests cling to steep mountainsides overlooking finger-like fjords. This area is known as the Northern Pacific Range and Kitimat Range Ecosections. Continuing inland, the mountains become extremely rugged, typified by Mount Saugstad, at 2,905 metres (9,532 feet) the highest mountain visible from the Bella Coola valley. This is the glacier-laden backbone of the Coast Mountains, which stretches along the western edge of British Columbia from the Fraser River delta to Alaska. In this area, coniferous forest cover is restricted to the lower elevations and most large watersheds consist of rock, ice and subalpine vegetation. East of the Coast Mountains the landscape quickly changes to the rolling hills of the Western Chilcotin Ranges and Upland Ecosections, which comprise the western part of the relatively flat Chilcotin Plateau.

Formation of the Coast Mountains

The Coast Mountains are a product of plate tectonics active on the western edge of North America for more than two billion years. The last volcanoes erupted in the Coast Mountains 14 to 11 million years ago. The Coast Mountains surrounding Bella Coola are granitic in composition and were formed by uplift of bedrock between two million and nine million years ago; pockets of sedimentary rocks contain fossils up to 170 million years old. (Many of these fossils are from marine animals, indicating that the host sediments were below sea level.) A major fault line runs through the Bella Coola valley, dividing the jagged Coast Mountains' Northern Pacific Ranges south of the valley from the older, more rounded Kitimat Ranges to the north.

Glaciers sculpted the Coast Mountains further during the great ice ages 1.7 million to 12,000 years ago. Some of the remaining icefields, such as the Monarch and Ha-iltzuk, are among the largest in subpolar North America. The glaciers today are only small remnants of past ice ages, but their rock-pulverizing power is still visible in the meltwater silt that gives many coastal rivers their cloudy turquoise colour. Plumes of this glacial river silt are evident far out into the ocean fjords, such as North Bentinck Arm, during the summer melt.

The continuous processes of mountain weathering are visible all around the Bella Coola landscape. In the spring and fall, the crack and thunder of distant avalanches and rockslides can be heard echoing in the tributary valleys. Large fans of rocky material (colluviums) are deposited at the toes of the mountains. This eroded material is pushed along and broken down by valley glaciers or fast-flowing creeks and rivers. Eventually it forms the gravel habitats necessary to support the many species of salmon and trout found in these rivers.

Following pages: Mad Dog Mountain on the left and Orbital Spire on the right. Extreme skiers ski down the middle chute of Mad Dog Mountain.

Pages 28-29: Alpenglow on School House Mountain.

Below: Table Top Mountain, a windswept peak of Mt. Stupendous.

A Magnificent Landscape

Above:
The view to the south
from Nusatsum Mountain.

Page 30:
Thorsen Creek valley.
Eagles frequently perch
here in winter months to
catch some warmth from
the sun as it passes for a
few brief hours through
this southern "notch" in
the mountains.

Page 31:
Coast Mountains have
some of the world's
largest subarctic
glaciers.

Mountaineering

Bella Coola is a rock climbers' and mountaineers' dream. From the bottom of the Hill to Firvale there are countless cliffs, boulders and faces within easy access from the side of the road to challenge climbers at every skill level. The mountain walls and faces surrounding Hagensborg are smoother and have longer pitches, similar to the walls surrounding Squamish.

To a large extent the Coast Mountains are still an unexplored frontier. Although climbers have reached the tops of the highest mountains, there are innumerable peaks yet to be named, let alone climbed. Breaking new trails is extremely demanding work and no one deserves more credit for unlocking the mountaineering mysteries of the Coast Mountains than the husband and wife team of Don and Phyl Munday.

From the 1920s to the 1950s, the Mundays climbed most of the major peaks in British Columbia and Alberta, many of them first ascents. Phyl's accomplishments at a time when mountaineering was a decidedly male pursuit were truly groundbreaking, and it is doubtful that many of the expeditions would have succeeded without her relentlessly cheerful approach to adversity. The Mundays' lifelong obsession was the mystery mountain, now known as Mount Waddington, but they climbed in the Bella Coola area as well, ascending Stupendous Mountain in 1936. Their descriptions of myriad peaks enticed other mountaineers to the area. The climbing boom of the early 1950s brought successful ascents of prominent peaks, including glacier-clad Mount

Saugstad, the highest peak visible from the Bella Coola valley, and Nusatsum Mountain.

At 2,423 metres (7,950 feet) Nusatsum may not rate as a major peak, but its jagged southern ridge of crumbling pillars and menacing summit tower give this mountain the dramatic qualities of mountaineering legend. According to First Nations mythology, when the Great Flood engulfed the world, the peak of Nusatsum Mountain was the only place left to tether the great life-saving canoe. The rope that held the canoe to the mountaintop can still be seen from the valley floor on certain frosty days, as a white horizontal line on the summit tower.

The most challenging part of climbing the Coast Mountains is not necessarily the imposing granite walls or razor-sharp ridges. It is the difficult slog through thick coastal forest just to reach the base of the chosen mountain. "For sheer exercise there is nothing that can compare with the pushing, pulling and stumbling through this green barricade of leaves and thorns with an 80-pound pack," says John Dundra, describing his ordeal en route to Mount Saugstad. Few know this better than John Baldwin, who hiked, climbed and skied his way from Bella Coola to the Fraser Valley in a series of trips starting in the 1970s and continuing to 1992. Realizing the difficulty in travelling below treeline, Baldwin carefully chose routes that linked ridges, mountaintops and icefields. In so doing, he probably documented more first ascents in the Coast Mountains than any other person, except possibly his climbing partner John Clark. But, as Baldwin points out in his book *Mountains of the Coast* (Harbour, 1999), "the impetus for a trip [into the mountains] has come to have less to do with accomplishing certain routes or first ascents, and more to do with the joy and excitement of visiting the high, wild and beautiful places that I have come to know so well. It is a simple, uncomplicated enjoyment of nature and its hidden treasures. It is the silence, the mist hanging over jagged peaks, the curves of snow on slopes as they recede into the distance, the waterfalls coursing down mossy outcrops of rock."

With some of the highest snowfalls and fewest skiers in North America, these heli-skiers enjoy a virtually limitless supply of untracked snow.

Climate—Liquid Sunshine

With annual rainfalls that can exceed four metres (160 inches) in maritime areas, coastal British Columbia is known for its wet climate. Most of this rain occurs during the winter, but the summers also receive rain showers and foggy drizzle that can last for days.

The level of rainfall on the western outer coast is dramatically different from that on the eastern flanks of the Coast Mountains because of the extreme mountain topography. Bella Coola, located smack in the centre of the coast, is often expected to be drearily wet. However, as the clouds push across the Coast Mountains, they are literally wrung dry, resulting in a "rain shadow" on the eastern side of the mountain chain. This rain shadow gives Bella Coola, which is more than 120 kilometres (70 miles) from the open ocean, a much drier climate than might be expected. The eastern end of the Bella Coola valley receives less than 30 centimetres (12 inches) of rain during the summer. The climate there is similar to some of the drier forested areas in the BC Interior. This pronounced east-west rain gradient creates a tremendous variety of flora and fauna over a short distance.

The wet coastal climate also keeps temperatures relatively mild by Canadian standards. Summers are generally pleasant, with temperatures in the high teens Celsius

An eagle is perched near the confluence of the Nusatsum and Bella Coola Rivers in late winter as the mist rises from the valley below.

(mid-60s Fahrenheit) on the coast and in the mid-20s Celsius (mid-70s Fahrenheit) inland.

In the Bella Coola valley, growing conditions are ideal, with alluvial soils and long daylight hours in summer. Just about everything can be grown here—even peaches. "We're in Zone 5 for plant hardiness," says June Vosburgh, a local nursery keeper. "Plants with warmer Zone 6 tolerances can be grown as well, but they need protection during cold snaps." Gardeners follow the North American rule of thumb of planting their garden on the May long weekend. If they start before that time, they risk late-season frost damage. If they plant later, the fall crop might not mature before frosts reappear.

During the winter, beginning in late November, temperatures hover around freezing at sea level. Snow comes and goes. The mountainous areas are a world of ice and snow from November to early April. Harsh winter conditions descend on the Central Coast for a few weeks in January and February when "outflow winds" roar down the valleys and inlets. Outflow winds occur when a high-pressure system from the Arctic parks itself over the BC Interior. The frigid air drains down from the Chilcotin plateau, gaining momentum until the coastal valleys and fjords become deadly wind tunnels that have caused more than a few tragic boat accidents. Even though the skies are sunny, temperatures drop to minus 15 Celsius (four degrees Fahrenheit). Storm-force winds easily drop the wind chill to 45 below zero—in either scale. This is not a good time to be travelling, especially by air or water. Better to stay inside, stoke the fire and curl up with a good book.

Down in the Bella Coola valley, the total annual snowfall ranges from one to two metres (three to six feet) but comes and goes intermittently through the winter, staying longer toward the colder east end of the valley. On the surrounding peaks, snow can occur at just about any time of the year and reaches great depths. Snow gates on the road by the Bella Coola wharf are closed when the avalanche danger is too high. At these times, explosives are dropped by helicopter to trigger avalanches.

Many residents of the Bella Coola valley become acutely aware of the therapeutic benefit of the sun during the winter. At this time the low-arching sun reaches the valley bottom at only a few locations. People watch in dread as mountain shadows expand their reach in the fall, and count the days until the sun climbs over the obstructing mountains to once again bathe the valley in glorious sunshine.

Winter sunset on the Chilcotin.

CHAPTER 2

From Fire Forest to Rain Forest

Previous pages:
The Big Cedar tree at Larso Bay, a Bella Coola landmark. It takes 15 grade six students to reach all the way around this giant.

Above:
One of the many birds to return in the spring is the red-breasted sapsucker. The males tap incessantly on anything metal—tin roofs, metal ladders, drainpipes, etc.

Below:
Dry forest in the Chilcotin.

One of the most striking ways to experience the diversity of British Columbia's forests is to drive to Bella Coola along Highway 20 from Williams Lake in the BC Interior. This route takes travellers through a variety of dry Interior forests until its dramatic descent into the Bella Coola valley, where the coastal climate gives rise to imposing rain forests.

Williams Lake is dry, and it becomes even drier on the descent to lower elevations along the Fraser River. At Farwell Canyon on the Chilcotin River, desert conditions exist. As you move west across the Chilcotin plateau, the ecology quickly changes to grassy ranch country broken by Douglas fir woodlands. This in turn gives way to a vast expanse of trembling aspen and lodgepole pine (jack pine) forests interspersed with Engelmann spruce along riverbanks and wetland areas.

As the elevation increases beyond Anahim Lake, the sweet fragrance of subalpine fir begins to permeate the air. In the cooler forests of the Engelmann spruce/subalpine fir zone found in Tweedsmuir Park, differing hues of green reflect a varied ecology consisting of a mix of subalpine ponds and wetland complexes surrounded by thick timber stands. This forest continues to the edge of the Chilcotin plateau, where the infamous "Hill" marks the dramatic change from flat vistas to the vertical relief of the Coast Mountains.

Above:
The East Chilcotin landscape in the Alexis Creek area.

Left:
Subalpine forest landscape.

Above:
Valuable pine mushrooms have become a welcome source of revenue in the Bella Coola valley.

Below:
A pair of bald eagles perch on black cottonwood.

As you descend the Hill, the stick-like trees of the plateau give way to gnarly old Douglas fir that cling to the dry, rock-strewn slopes. Once you reach the bottom, a sense of relief at having made it down in one piece combines with a feeling of comfort as you enter a deep forest nestled below spectacular mountain peaks. Gone is the open but arid Chilcotin. In its place a canopy of towering Douglas fir, western red cedar and black cottonwood trees exudes a cool serenity. This forest is still more Interior than coastal, but it is a sign of things to come.

Continuing west toward Bella Coola, the road traverses the Coast Mountain rain shadow. The eastern flanks of the Coast Mountains support a narrow band of Interior Douglas fir. Here the forest floor is sparsely covered with prince's pine, twin-flower, step moss and electrified cat's tail moss. Paper birch and the odd Douglas maple also appear, adding to a spectacular autumn display of yellow and green with smatterings of orange. When the fall rains arrive, mushrooms begin to emerge from the forest floor. This is where the prized pine mushroom thrives, attracting hundreds of pickers during its fall fruiting phase.

Gradually, western hemlock begins to dominate the forests, a sign that the climate is getting wetter. Red alder is now common along riverbanks, roadsides and other disturbed areas. Shrubs and herbs are more prolific. Alaskan blueberry is common under the tree canopies while thimbleberry and salmonberry thrive in more open areas. Nearer the ocean, the forest begins to take on the ethereal character of temperate rain forests, where long strands of cat-tail moss, common witch's hair and speckled horsehair lichen hang from tree branches that are often shrouded in mist. Giant Sitka spruce, with their large root buttresses, are prominent on the floodplain and wet areas.

The Bella Coola River meets the ocean at the head of North Bentinck Arm, which leads west from the submaritime zone to the wetter maritime zone. Even though the submaritime transition forest appears lush and moist, dry summer conditions can create extreme fire hazards. Forests in this area burn every 200 years or so. Douglas fir, with its thick fire-resistant bark, can tolerate light surface fires and

Page 41:
Douglas fir forest in spring near Tweedsmuir Lodge.

Opposite:
Sitka spruce thrives in fertile bottomland.

Above:
Shaggy mane mushrooms in the drier eastern half of the Bella Coola valley.

Below:
Clouds rising through the lower reaches of Nusatsum Mountain.

From Fire Forest to Rain Forest

Jenny Falls, King Island, west of Bella Coola. A landscape dominated by cedar-hemlock rain forest.

most old Douglas firs bear the blackened bark of past fires. Once every 200 years on average, catastrophic stand-replacing fires clear tracts of forest in a single pass, thus creating conditions in which shade-intolerant pioneer species, such as fireweed and Douglas fir, are able to establish. They grow into a forest that is evenly aged except for strips along rivers and creeks that usually do not burn. As the forest matures, shade-tolerant species such as hemlock and cedar are able to grow under the canopy cover and take over unless fire restarts the cycle.

Nusatsum and Clayton Falls logging roads in Bella Coola take you high into the subalpine areas, where stunted mountain hemlock, subalpine fir and yellow cedar are the only trees able to survive alongside the pink and white mountain heather. Above the treeline, a complex of springy carpeted heaths and meadows are a hiker's joy, especially in August when the countless alpine flowers are in full bloom. Farther up into the inhospitable but spectacular world of rock, ice and snow, only a few hardy plants such as moss campion and lichen are able to survive.

Above:
Moss campion, found in the alpine areas.

Right:
Red mountain heather, an alpine species.

Opposite:
View near the summit of the Nusatsum valley logging road.

West of Bella Coola lies a maze of mountains and fjords. This is the heart of the coastal rain forest, where prolific vegetation attests to the soggy weather. Abundant rain, mild temperatures, long growing season and good drainage make the Central Coast rain forest extremely productive. Despite the nutrient-poor soils, young conifers easily grow more than a metre (three feet) per year to reach heights of more than 70 metres (230 feet) at maturity. Shrub and herb complexes are highly developed, with a rich diversity of salmonberry, devil's club, huckleberries and blueberries. These combine with deer fern, five-leaved bramble, bunchberry and fern-leaved goldthread. Virtually everything is covered with green vegetation, including the forest floor, where step moss and lanky moss spread out like a wall-to-wall carpet. In places where sunlight is able to reach the ground through the tall timbers, brush growth of devil's club, salmonberry and various blueberries is so prolific that its density rivals that of tropical forests. Among the most inspiring aspects of the coastal rain forest is its age. Long-lived species such as red cedar can survive for more than 1,000 years, although most large

Previous pages:
A remnant of the old-growth forest in the lower Bella Coola valley at Walker Island Park.

Above:
A gnarly old cedar personifies the rain forest mystique.

Right:
The hairy woodpecker can be found year-round in the Bella Coola valley.

rainforest trees range in age from 200 to 500 years. The coastal rain forests themselves, however, can be much older. Recent studies have indicated that forest-replacing fires have not occurred in some Central Coast forests since their birth after the last ice age some 10,000 years ago. Due to the long time between stand-destroying events, the slow decomposition rate and long-lived tree species, these ecosystems are among the most massive on earth.

Dead and decaying wood, which makes up almost half of the biomass in ancient forests, supports complex communities of organisms. In fact, most of the biodiversity in the temperate rain forest is found underfoot. A single square metre of rainforest duff (the uppermost soil level) can host hundreds of thousands of tiny springtails and mites and millions of nematodes or worms. Thousands more microorganisms dwell in the leaves, needles and mossy limbs of the overhead canopy. The role these tiny organisms play in the cycling of forest nutrients is just now starting to be explored.

Left:
Cedar trees in a jungle of devil's club.

Top to bottom:
Red elderberry berries; mountain lady's slipper; fairy slipper.

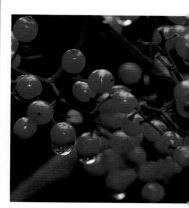

To Log or Not to Log

Opponents of logging point to the mass and diversity of the ancient rain forest as qualities that are lost when the stands are cut over, then reforested and later reharvested on a 60-to-120-year cycle. Old-growth forests take much longer to mature and therefore, opponents argue, traditional stand removal by logging prevents rainforest succession from ever reaching its climax phase. Supporters of logging point out that productive rain forests recover quickly from disturbances like logging. Some argue that after only 80 years the forest starts to take on characteristics of old growth, with canopy gaps, multiple tree layers and plant associations similar to the original forest. At the heart of this debate is the question of balance between ensuring the sustainability of the rainforest ecosystem with the economic needs of communities.

It is in the hope of resolving this issue that the Central Coast Land and Resource Management Planning (CCLRMP) has been carrying out one of the most intensive planning initiatives in the world. Through a commitment to Ecosystem Based Management by all the parties, there is optimism that they can ensure the old-growth coastal rain forest will be around forever and communities will be able to support their needs.

Above:
A faller pauses in his work. Fallers come first into areas slated for logging and fall the trees, making it one of the most dangerous jobs in the country.

Right:
A naturally regenerated cutover in South Bentinck Arm that was logged in the early 1910s.

Opposite:
The Atnarko, the most productive salmon river on the Central Coast.

Above:
Trumpeter swans arrive in the Bella Coola estuary by late December and stay until late March or early April.

Below:
Peep sandpipers travel through the Bella Coola area in spring and autumn.

Key Rainforest Niche Habitats

Rainforest diversity is further enriched by the variety of smaller niche habitats that result from variations in soil fertility, drainage and topography. Bogs and fens are permanently wet ecosystems with anaerobic soil conditions that slow the rate of decomposition, producing deep, black organic soils. These ecosystems host some of the rarer plants, such as the insect-eating round-leaved sundew, as well as more common species like the ubiquitous skunk cabbage.

The richest ecosystems usually occur where land and water meet. Along the banks of rivers and streams, disturbances are frequent due to flooding and natural erosion. The constant seepage of nutrients, often enhanced by waste left by animals feeding on spawning salmon, make these areas highly fertile. Here delicate stalks of foamflower can be seen intermingling with lady fern and saxifrage.

Estuaries are key habitats linking marine and terrestrial ecosystems. Grasses and sedges flourish in these deltas with their fine-textured soils and brackish water. Juvenile salmon spend a critical part of their life cycle in estuaries, adjusting to higher salinity and feeding on the rich nutrients in preparation for their long migration into the open ocean.

Some ecosystems stay at one stage of development due to continuous disturbances. In brushy avalanche tracks, yearly snow slides prevent trees from growing, so the underbrush is never shaded out by a tree canopy. Mountain goats, deer and bears seek out these fertile sites for herbs, berry bushes and such plants as cow parsnip and sweet cicely.

Continuing west toward the open ocean, the mountains diminish in size and the shoreline becomes more intricate as fjords give way to a sprawling archipelago. Gone are the snow-capped mountains. In their place, rolling hills are completely covered by slow-growing red cedar and hemlock forests. On the outer coast, the topography tapers down until it is nearly flat. Bogs and wetlands abound and poor drainage stunts tree growth. Shoreline trees often assume a bonsai-like appearance. Here, lodgepole pine, Sitka spruce and yellow cedar struggle to survive among sphagnum moss, salal, Alaskan blueberry, Labrador tea and false azalea. Bird life is especially rich as the outer coast is situated along one of the great North American bird migration routes.

Above:
Gulls congregate in Rivers Inlet during the many salmon runs between August and October.

Left:
Wood ducks breed in the Walker Island beaver ponds.

Right:
Skunk cabbage provides the first colour to be seen in early spring and is one of the first plants foraged by bears.

Far right:
Round-leaved sundew, a carnivorous plant found in lower elevation bogs.

Below:
Southwest of King Island, the topography tapers down.

First Nations Use of Forest Resources

Although most of their protein came from the sea, the Nuxalk people of Bella Coola also hunted such forest creatures as deer, mountain goat, small animals and game birds. (When used as a noun to refer to the Nuxalk people, the form "Nuxalkmc," pronounced *noohalkum*, is used; when used as an adjective, "Nuxalk," pronounced *noo-halk*, is used.) The hunter, who regarded both man and animal as immortal, believed his quarry would discard its worthless blanket of flesh and give it to the respectful hunter as its spirit ascended. In the 1920s, anthropologist T.F. McIlwraith observed: "Success as a hunter therefore, does not indicate mastery over an animal, so much as the latter's goodwill in allowing itself to be slain by one who has pleased him by ceremonial chastity." That belief continues today. Hereditary chief Andy Siwallace says he has learned that "You got to give lots of respect to every animal in the woods, they can sense it."

Certain seaweeds were eaten, but forest plants provided most of the nutrient variety needed for a balanced diet. It is estimated that aboriginal peoples used more than 130 species of plants as food or flavourings and several hundred more for medicines. Still more plants were transformed into material goods that display a high level of craftsmanship. Following the cycles of nature, different plants and plant parts were harvested according to the season. In early spring, when the sap flows in the trees, the edible cambium and inner bark were shaved from hemlock, cottonwood and red alder trees.

Above:
First Nations hunted forest birds such as grouse.

Below:
Black-tailed deer are hard to spot in the forest.

All kinds of berries were picked as they ripened in succession throughout the growing season, beginning with salmonberries and wild strawberries in late May. Elderberries, huckleberries, blueberries and thimbleberries, to name a few, were picked in mid-summer, followed by currants and gooseberries. Eva Mack, a former teacher and local expert on traditional plant uses, recalls that "people didn't just walk around the bush looking for berries. They often cultivated suitable patches by routinely burning small areas to keep berry patches from getting overgrown with trees." Tart crabapples, cranberries and soapberries were picked in fall along with rosehips. These were stored in water or oil to soften and sweeten them for winter consumption. The berries were eaten fresh in season, and many were preserved for later use by cooking them into a jam-like pulp that was then dried into cakes. During hot summer days, berries were also laid out to dry like raisins.

Succulent new shoots such as fiddlehead ferns were picked in springtime and eaten fresh. Many of the other vegetable foods consisted of roots. Bulbs from the lily family and wild onions were dug up, as were the roots of plants such as spiny wood fern and lupines. These were harvested later in the season, when the plant's leaves were beginning to die back. Mushrooms were rarely used.

Traditional healers used a considerable pharmacopoeia of plants to make ointments, teas, compresses and washing solutions to treat a variety of ailments. Tree pitch, mashed leaves and solutions made from special plants were applied to injuries. Different roots or leaves were chewed to treat sore throat. Most internal ailments were treated by drinking teas, while sore eyes—common in the smoky longhouses—were treated with soothing solutions. Dr. Harvey Thommasen, a local physician and naturalist, has documented 75 plant species used by the Nuxalkmc; some plants, such as devil's club, had such potent cures that they were linked to spiritual beliefs. The root of the Indian hellebore is also powerful, for it contains unstable alkaloid poisons. "Not only does it relieve sore muscles and arthritic pain," says Nuxalk elder Lillian Siwallace, "it also keeps out evil spirits." Hellebore was traditionally hung over the house door, and was often grated into bathwater. Scientific study is starting to confirm the medicinal qualities of plants such as devil's club, whose antibacterial properties and compounds have beneficial effects on blood glucose. Other examples include Pacific yew tree bark, which contains taxol, a powerful cancer-fighting drug, and red alder, an antibiotic.

Plants were also the raw material for a diverse technology. The large, thick leaves of the skunk cabbage were used to line steam pits and berry baskets. Hard branch-knot wood from dead hemlock trees was heated and bent into fish hooks. The easily hollowed-out stems of red elderberry were used for pipe stems and straws, the extremely hard wood from yew and crabapple for implement handles, bows, wedges and digging sticks. Dried cottonwood roots yielded drills and hearths for making friction fires. The fibre from stinging nettles was dried, pounded and spun into twine for fishing nets. Various dyes were extracted from the bark of hemlock and red alder. Birch bark was made into baskets.

Cedars—Trees of Life

Beautiful in shape, with giant tapering trunks leading to a crown of lazy fronds covered with scale-like needles, western red cedar is the most cherished tree species on the Central Coast. Its wood is straight-grained, resistant to rot, easy to work and pleasingly fragrant. Cedar, or *tsatswalhp*, is revered for its central role in coastal First Nations society. Cedar can easily survive injury that would kill other species. It is possible to remove planks from large cedar trees by cutting a notch at the base of the tree and another notch at the desired plank length, then splitting planks from the trunk with wedges of bone, stone or yew. With only a portion of its stem removed, the resilient cedar can live for centuries. Traditionally the men worked with the tree's wood, while women wove the stringy bark fibres into mats, baskets and clothing. Collected from live trees, the bark was removed from only one-third of the circumference of the tree so as not to girdle its trunk. Scars left from "cultural modifications" such as test holes, planking or bark stripping done hundreds of years ago can still be seen in living trees today. Culturally modified trees provide hard evidence of aboriginal land-use patterns and history.

Opposite page, top to bottom:
Field of lupine, gooseberry, twinberry, salmonberry.

Above:
Western red cedar is recognized by its scaly needles.

Left:
The Hawhaw bird mask, carved by Tony Speers. Cedar provided First Nations with the ideal carving medium.

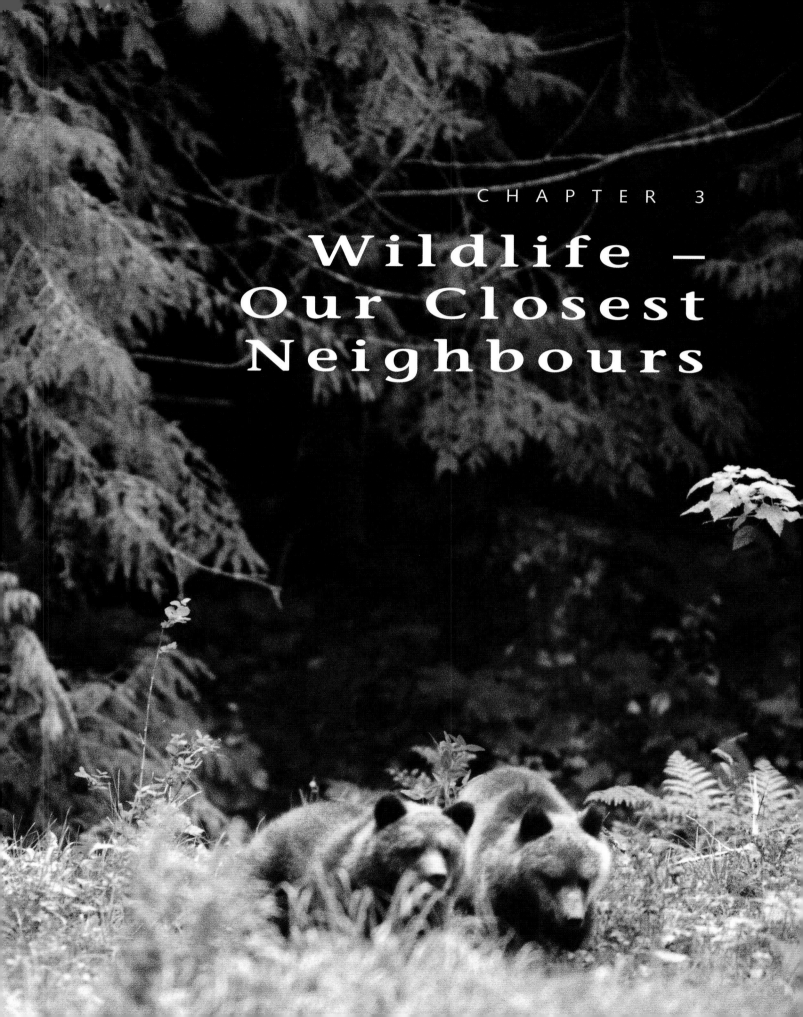

CHAPTER 3

Wildlife – Our Closest Neighbours

One of the greatest attractions of the Central Coast is the abundance of wildlife. Roaming this untamed landscape are the majestic animals of the North American wilderness—grizzly bears, black bears, kermode bears, cougars, wolves, mountain goats, deer and bald eagles—the entire list would fill pages. These wildlife populations are relatively healthy because of plentiful habitat. Although they prefer the unsettled areas, it is not uncommon to see large mammals in the backyards of Bella Coola homes, munching on flowers, raiding vegetable gardens or fruit orchards and agitating household pets. These close encounters stir mixed feelings of dread and delight.

Previous pages:
Grizzly sow with two cubs.

Above:
The water dipper can be seen around fast-moving streams.

Below:
Seals relax on the sun-warmed rocks of Labouchere Channel.

Opposite:
Pikas inhabit high-elevation talus slopes.

Living with Grizzly Bears

Unrivalled in size and strength, the grizzly bear is king of the coastal forest. It has a ferocious reputation as old as the dawn of humanity and was feared by Natives and settlers alike as they struggled to share its wilderness domain. The Nuxalkmc called the grizzly *nan* and sought to acquire its strength and courage through ritual. Grizzlies range in colour from pale yellow to dark brown and nearly black. The hairs of the coat are often lightly tipped, giving a frosted or "grizzled" appearance.

The variety of productive habitats found in the Central Coast makes this area ideal for omnivorous animals such as grizzly bears. Having evolved from a predatory species, the grizzly now survives for much of the year on vegetation. The first signs that bears have emerged from their winter dens, usually in April, are the telltale excavations in swamps and wetland areas where they have been digging up skunk cabbage roots. These pungent plants help to kick-start the bears' digestive rhythm. As the snow continues to melt, grizzlies feed on emerging grass, sedge, horsetail and fiddlehead fern shoots. These plants are found in lowland meadows, swamps, tide flats and at mid-elevations in brushy avalanche tracks.

Clayton Mack

For almost 50 years, the legendary grizzly bear guide Clayton Mack led the rich and famous on hunting expeditions throughout Bella Coola country. Son of Nuxalk chief Willie Mack and grandson of Hudson's Bay Company trader John Clayton, he was the

personification of Bella Coola history, a man in whom the area's First Nations and European traditions entwined. He was an entertaining storyteller around the campfire. "I see over 300 grizzly bears get killed," Clayton says. "I only shot the ones that tried to kill me or the wounded ones, that's all." Clayton's success rate did not come without close brushes with death himself. Once, with a griz pinning his shoulders to the ground, Clayton recalled how the bear "put her nose right in my face. Kind of smell me, snorting like. Saliva coming out of her mouth. I could smell that old rotten fish breath."

Another time, Clayton demonstrated his characteristic "Bella Cool" while trapped below an overhanging riverbank by an enraged young griz and surrounded by stinging yellow jackets. Clayton "was scared to move too much. If I run that grizzly bear will get me; if I stay, I get stung. Then he came down, slide down, in an awkward way, like. He came down with his head down and then I see his jaw. I just about touch him, then I pull the trigger of that short .350 magnum rifle. Bang! He keep still there, I think I got him." In the twilight of his years and confined to a hospital bed in Bella Coola, Clayton told his life story to his physician, Dr. Harvey Thommasen, who worked with his wife Carol to transcribe Clayton's tales into the popular *Grizzlies and White Guys: The Stories of Clayton Mack* (Harbour, 1993).

Above:
Fox and large grizzly boar squaring off over a morsel. A second later, the bear was chasing the fox around the meadow and the fox, living up to its wily reputation, doubled back, grabbed the food and bolted into the woods.

Left:
Grizzly in profile.

During the summer, bears forage in all parts of their range. They feed on insects, carrion and small mammals as the opportunity arises. From early summer on, however, they devour the changing buffet of blackberry, elderberry, salmonberry, thimbleberry, huckleberry, blueberry and devil's club. It is easy to surprise a bear in a thicket of ripe berry bushes, so pickers are well advised to use extreme caution and make lots of noise. Bear sign—piles of fresh dung—can usually be counted on to provide warning of a bear's presence.

Besides droppings, there are many other signs that demonstrate the presence of bears. Trails that are used frequently are often "padded" with a chain of paw tracks up to 15 centimetres (six inches) deep, resulting from grizzly bears' ritualistic habit of stepping in the same exact place over and over. Along rivers and natural travel corridors, it is also common to see teeth and claw marks left on signpost trees. Bear bathtubs, or mud wallows, are used in swampy areas during hot summer months.

As the salmon start to migrate upriver to their spawning grounds, grizzly bears begin a heavy feeding cycle to fatten up for winter. Grizzlies can have home ranges of more than 80 square kilometres (30 square miles) and are generally solitary animals, but during salmon season they often congregate along major rivers. At first they are picky, mainly eating the eggs in pre-spawn salmon. Later in the fall they feed on the putrid meat of the spawned-out salmon. Bears feeding on this culinary delight will take on its distinctive smell—so be careful if you come across a fishy aroma in the middle of the woods.

Opposite:
Grizzly cubs on the Neechans River. These young bears search the shoreline of a back eddy pool for salmon carcasses. An osprey looks on from an overhanging alder tree.

Below:
Grizzly keeps watch from mid-river perch.

Wildlife — Our Closest Neighbours

Above:
Over a million pink salmon return to the Bella Coola watershed each year, making it a prime draw for grizzlies.

Right:
A second-year grizzly cub crosses a river channel to meet up with mom.

Opposite:
Grizzly searching for sockeye on the Neechans River in the Owikeno system.

Following pages:
A grizzly grasps a chinook salmon on the Atnarko River.

The best deterrent

Bob Lenci, a retired forester and gentleman gardener, has discovered an ingenious way of keeping bears out of his fruit trees. When he hangs a transistor radio in his orchard, he finds that bears no longer wander in to fill up on fruit. Bob has found that "the best deterrent isn't rock music, but the regular programming on CBC Radio."

The radio trick didn't save Bob's pool, though. "This young griz had decided to take a cooling dip in my pool one time and when I tried to scare him out, his claws ripped the lining to shreds as he was trying to climb out of the deep end."

The best way to minimize midnight raids is to pick orchard fruit just before it ripens. Or enlist the services of a trusty dog to sound the alarm when an unwelcome garden robber appears.

In Bella Coola grizzly bears like to supplement their usual diet by raiding vegetable gardens and fruit orchards. Many local gardeners have gone out into the dewy morning air to find steaming piles of bear manure next to their newly roto-tilled vegetable gardens. Even though grizzly bears seem to eat anything, including oil and gas jugs, in our garden they will not touch the tomatoes. Of more concern is their unceremonious pruning of favourite fruit trees.

Apart from the salmon runs, the only occasions on which grizzlies socialize is the mating season in May and June. Sows usually breed every three or four years. Depending on population densities, females may mate with more than one male, which can result in litters with cubs from different fathers. Cubs are born in the den in January or February, in litters that usually consist of two cubs. Occasionally three cubs emerge with the mother. The cubs are weaned by late summer but stay with their mother through the next two seasons.

Because male bears and wolves occasionally kill cubs, nature has endowed female grizzlies with the ability to call up extremely aggressive behaviour when protecting their young. To escape danger, cubs will run away from threats and occasionally climb trees. Cubs have curved claws that allow them to scurry up tree trunks. Adult grizzly claws lose their curvature, making it hard for the bear to scale a trunk, although it will sometimes climb a tree with thick limbs. Coastal grizzlies are the largest in Canada, with adult males ranging from 300 to 400 kilograms (650 to 850 pounds) and the occasional giant weighing more than 450 kilograms (1,000 pounds). Sows generally weigh a third less.

Grizzly bears evolved in open habitat during the Pleistocene epoch, when large, now-extinct predators such as the sabre-tooth tiger were capable of killing them. To

Opposite:
A mother grizzly and her second-year cub. This is usually the last year the cub will have the advantage of living with its mother.

Below:
Healthy grizzly sows often manage to rear two cubs, occasionally three.

Following pages:
The large grizzly boar is lord of the rain forest.

Wildlife – Our Closest Neighbours

defend against these ferocious enemies, grizzlies developed a behaviour pattern of threatening animals with false charges and, when necessary, real attacks. This ingrained defensive-aggressive behaviour is still preva-lent in grizzly bears. As Gary Shelton points out in his book, *Bear Encounter Survival Guide* (1997), under-standing this behaviour is key to minimizing contact, which can be fatal to both human and bear.

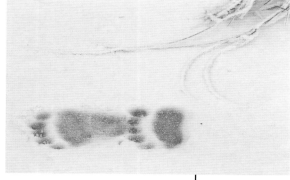

The grizzly bear's range in North America is now greatly reduced as a result of expanding human popu-lation, habitat alienation and deliberate eradication during previous centuries. The status of grizzly popu-lations in British Columbia is a controversial topic. Government biologists estimate that there are approxi-mately 14,000 grizzlies in the province, while some independent biologists argue the figure is closer to 4,000. Some studies rate the viability of grizzly populations as good to excellent on the Central Coast, but others state that populations are not sustain-able under present conditions. Sightings are so commonplace in the Bella Coola val-ley that the local population appears to be thriving.

Opposite:
Portrait of a black bear.

Above:
Apart from their size, you can tell grizzly tracks by the long claw marks set well apart from the toes.

Below:
Two black bears skirmish at the edge of a clearing.

Black Bears and Spirit Bears

The black bear, a distant relative of the grizzly, is more common throughout British Columbia and on the Central Coast. Generally smaller, black bears, or *tl'a* in the Nuxalk language, can be further distinguished from grizzlies by the lack of a promi-nent shoulder hump. They also have a straight nose rather than the slightly upturned profile of the grizzly bear. The footprints of black bears can usually be distinguished

by the position of the claw marks in relation to the toe imprint. Black bear claws are shorter and more curved, while grizzly claws are long and straight, striking the ground some distance ahead of the toe print. The name black bear is something of a misnomer since *Ursus americanus* comes in a broad spectrum of colours from black to cinnamon to honey blonde to the uncommon white phase known as the kermode or spirit bear.

As white as a polar bear, the kermode bear has a mystical, ghost-like presence in the rain forest. According to one First Nations legend, after Raven melted the ice and snow and turned the earth green, he created the spirit bear as a reminder of the world's beauty when all was white. It was Dr. Francis Kermode, a former director of the provincial museum, who collected the white pelts that eventually led to the scientific classification of this distinctive strain in 1905. The kermode is not a separate

Opposite:
The kermode bear is a normal black bear except for its white coat.

Below:
If this bear had black eyes and nose it would be a kermode, but its pinkish-orange nose and pale pinkish-blue eyes identify it as an albino black bear.

species. Nor is it an albino. It is actually a typical black bear in every respect except the colour of its fur. White is just another of the black bear's many coat variants, but the gene that carries it is recessive, which causes it to manifest very rarely. But in the coastal subpopulation centred on Princess Royal Island it occurs a whopping ten percent of the time. This has attracted much attention to this particular strain and generated strong efforts to protect it.

Nature's Mountaineer

High among the Coast Mountains lives the mountain goat, one of the most intriguing animals in North America. With its white cloak, tufted beard and black, slightly curved horns, the mountain goat lives among inhospitable peaks that effectively defend it from predators. In spring these goats can easily be seen in the Bella Coola valley, grazing on the cliffs directly above the highway at Firvale. As the season progresses, the goats move to higher, cooler elevations. Any but the fittest climber will need a spotting scope to see the goats as they escape the heat and bugs of summer.

To minimize falls, the mountain goat has specially adapted non-slip hooves, shaped like suction cups with hard rims and soft centres. Like any mountaineer, goats must still be careful not to misstep. They learn at an early age to place the rear foot exactly where the front foot found purchase. With musculature designed for climbing, mountain goats are distinctively heavy-shouldered, giving them the "white buffalo" appearance noted by the explorer Alexander Mackenzie in his journals in 1793.

Mountain goats, or *yaki* in the Nuxalk language, were a traditional source of wool for aboriginal weavers. In the spring, when the goats moulted their thick winter coats, people would climb up among the cliffs to collect tufts of fur from branches along goat trails and bedding areas. The wool was cleaned and spun for making blankets and clothing.

Goats are most vulnerable when they descend from their mountain ramparts to seek winter cover among the trees or to frequent salt licks in the valley. Wolves, mountain lions, bears and lynx will readily take goats at these locations.

Mountain goats are often seen in the most precarious locations with no visible route to safety. Rob Skelly, one of the most experienced helicopter bush pilots in the Coast Mountains, jokes, "They are born up here and simply can't get down." In fact, kids quickly learn how to manoeuvre around the cliffs. Ewes give birth in spring, six months after mating, and the newborns can stand within 10 minutes. After 30 minutes they are able to jump and follow their parents as if immune to gravity. Even so, the mortality rate among the young is high. Like children everywhere, goat kids are rambunctious as they hone their climbing skills. In the mountain goat's extreme habitat, a simple misplaced step can be fatal. Eagles are known to swoop down and knock young goats off ledges.

Opposite:
A mountain goat stands confidently on a rock face in the Firvale area.

Below:
A nanny mountain goat and her kid have made their way down from the valley walls to a salt lick near Firvale. It's midsummer and the nanny is shedding her coat.

Lord of the Skies

Sharing the mountain goat's lofty domain is *ts'lkt*, or bald eagle. This magnificent flyer figures prominently in First Nations culture—the eagle is one of the traditional family crests. A graceful glider, the bald eagle can detect the tiniest changes in air current with the finger-like feathers splayed at the tips of its wings. The bird's wingspan may reach 2.5 metres (eight feet). Eagle counts during the 1980s and 1990s in Bella Coola show that the overwintering population has been holding steady at around 250, of which 75 percent are mature adults.

The bald eagle is one of the most adaptable of all raptors and will eat many different things. Coastal eagles take seabirds in addition to a variety of fish. Farther inland, wildfowl and carrion supplement the salmon and trout diet. Generally not a hunter of small mammals, the bald eagle has been known to take otters. However, the main *modus operandi* is to swoop down from a waterside perch and snatch any fish idling too close to the surface. Sometimes an eagle hooks its claws into a fish that is too large to pull out of the water. Instead of letting go, the bird clumsily drags the fish to shore, using its wings as oars. After such a wet and tiring ordeal, a spent eagle will sit motionless on a perch with its wings half-spread to dry.

The best time to observe bald eagles is in late summer and fall, when river shores are littered with salmon carcasses and a dozen or more eagles may perch in the same tree overlooking a favourite feeding spot. Eagles subsist on these rotting fish well into winter, and although mature bald eagles are generally solitary, at this time of year they form communal roosts. Immature eagles, on the other hand, continue to stay in small groups throughout the summer. Younger eagles retain a scruffy brown plumage that gradually changes over four or five years to the clean white head and tail and dark body markings of the adult.

Bald eagles mate early in spring. Two, occasionally three, white eggs are laid in a massive nest—a tangle of sticks more than two metres (six feet) across—high in a wind-firm tree such as a cottonwood or Douglas fir. These nests are used year after year, and the trees bearing them are protected from logging; "no-work zones" are established around occupied trees until the chicks leave the nest. The female incubates the eggs with some help from the male, and if both leave the nest, the eggs are covered. The parents feed the offspring for 70 to 77 days but usually only one chick survives the competition for food.

Above:
A raven hungrily eyes the coho carcass claimed by a young eagle.

Below:
An eagle landing near a seal carcass washed ashore in the Bella Coola estuary.

Wildlife – Our Closest Neighbours

Above:
Eagles tug either end of a coho carcass on the iced banks of Thorsen Creek. Eventually the fish's spine breaks and each eagle flies off with a portion of the prize.

Right:
Coho can be found spawning in the Bella Coola tributaries as late as January, a great blessing to eagles in the lean winter months.

Opposite:
This eagle has found a scrap of frozen meat in the snow. After the salmon are gone and before the herring spawn occurs in early spring, eagles scavenge where they can.

Left:
An eagle soars through
the winter sky searching
for food.

Above:
Aided by keen vision, few
animals are better than
the eagle at the hunter's
art of vigilant waiting.

Salmon—Hub of the Cycle of Life

Chinook, sockeye, chum, pink and coho salmon and steelhead all migrate up the rivers of the Bella Coola area at different times of the year to spawn. In late May, when the Bella Coola River, fed by the melting snow, is at its highest flow, about 20,000 to 30,000 chinook or spring salmon (*amlh* to the Nuxalkmc) return to spawn. During the height of the run, from mid-June to early July, there is not much elbow room at some of the more popular fishing holes, where eager anglers hope to hook the largest of all Pacific salmon species. Adult chinook have been recorded at more than 40 kilograms (88 pounds), but the average weight is around 12 to 20 kilograms (25 to 45 pounds).

It takes patience, skill and endurance to land one of these magnificent fish, since a hooked salmon will use the power of the river current to multiply the weight pulling on a fisherman's line. It is not unusual for a muscle-cramped angler to struggle for nearly an hour trying to pull one of these lion-hearted fish to shore, only to lose it at the last minute as it torpedoes downstream in a thrashing explosion of energy.

Soon after the chinook enter the Bella Coola River, the sockeye begin their journey upriver to the Stillwater and Lonesome Lake chain in Tweedsmuir Park, where they rear their young. To commercial and Native food fishermen, the two-kilogram (four- to five-pound) sockeye, or *samlh*, is the most prized salmon because of its rich flavour and bright orange flesh.

The summer run of chum salmon (*t'li*) in the Bella Coola River averages from 60,000 to 110,000 adults, each weighing five to eight kilograms (11 to 18 pounds). These large schools are impressive sights as they stake out their mating sites in the various tributary streams in the lower part of the Bella Coola watershed. During the tourist season, there is often a "traffic jam" (by Bella Coola standards) at the Nooklikonnic Bridge crossing as travellers stop to witness all the commotion in the creek below.

Large schools of pink salmon adults crowd the holding pools of the Atnarko River in August. By early September they've moved upstream to their spawning grounds.

The most prolific salmon in the Bella Coola system is the pink, or *kap'ay*, with some runs estimated at more than two million fish. This huge influx of adult fish and resulting exodus of fry is a fundamental part of the ecology of the river system, often sustaining the other salmon species. In the spring, when the fry emerge, they provide a key food source for juvenile coho and chinook as well as for Dolly Varden, cutthroat trout and steelhead. During this time, a fry pattern on a fly rod makes for some great trout fishing. The smallest of the salmon, the pink weighs only one or two kilograms (two to five pounds).

August is the month for pinks in the Bella Coola River. The runs are so large that it is easy to catch these small salmon using light fishing gear and a hook baited only with a plastic salmon egg or red yarn. An ideal fish for the impatient fisherman, pinks are great for kids, who thrill at pulling these lively catches ashore. And although salmon connoisseurs may turn up their noses at pinks, a fresh bright pink on the barbecue is a real summer treat.

Coho, or *ways* in Nuxalk, is the mainstay for the marine sport fishery, especially in August. Averaging three to six kilograms (seven to 13 pounds), coho do not require the heavy-duty fishing gear needed to land chinook. Because the coho runs peak in the Bella Coola River from mid-September to mid-October, a lazy fisherman also does not need to get up as early to beat the sunrise crowd to a favourite fishing hole. In recent years, the run in the Bella Coola River has been averaging 30,000 to 35,000, although it varies greatly between years, with some runs as high as 79,000 and some as low as 7,500.

The sixth salmon species is the steelhead, or *k'lat*, which is actually a sea-run rainbow

Above:
In March and April, chum and pink fry emerge from spawning beds and migrate downstream. Chum fry have vertical "parr" marks on their sides. Pink fry are smaller and have no parr marks.

Below:
A coho male has made his way back to his natal stream.

Intent sport fishermen pursue Bella Coola coho in early autumn.

trout. Unlike the other salmon species, which die after spawning, steelhead may reproduce a number of times and return to sea in the intervals. This fish is one of the larger salmon, weighing up to 18 kilograms (40 pounds). Prized among anglers for its cunning and lively fight, it is identified by the spots on its upper body half, lines of spots on its tail and the lack of teeth at the back of the throat and tongue. Unfortunately, steelhead may not be taken from the Bella Coola River because of critically low returns, but the Dean River, the main river system north of Bella Coola, is known internationally for its run of summer steelhead, which is still holding strong. A number of wilderness lodges operate on the Dean and cater to a clientele of discriminating catch-and-release fishermen.

Salmon returns to the Bella Coola system are generally thought to be depressed from a historical perspective. The reason for the decline in fish stocks is not clear, but it is likely a combination of factors. Rearing habitat in the lower Bella Coola River has been significantly compromised during the past century by land development for farming, housing, industry, road construction, flood control dykes installed to protect these developments, and early logging. But salmonid populations are assisted by the Snootli Hatchery, which is successfully supplementing local chum, chinook, sockeye and coho populations by up to 40 percent. Although much work remains to

be done, it is to be hoped that fresh-water salmon habitat is on the road to recovery in the Bella Coola watershed.

The Dean River is world-renowned for its summer steelhead fishery. Strictly catch and release, it is about skill and conservation.

The Salmon People

Traditional life for coastal First Nations revolves around the seasons of the salmon. In May, when the *amlhtam* or spring salmon start arriving, the Nuxalk people hold a salmon festival to welcome the returning salmon and to celebrate their life-giving cycle. In the past, salmon were caught in the river using weirs made of piled rocks and sticks. As well, nets made from cedar-bark string were used. Today, nylon nets are used in the food fishery. To ensure that adequate stocks reach the spawning grounds, the Nuxalk First Nation's resource department allows net fishing on certain days of the week only.

Traditionally, salmon was prepared in many different ways. It was eaten fresh in season, usually barbecued on an open fire. For winter supplies it was smoked and dried in great quantities, then soaked and served with eulachon oil.

Cod and halibut were caught by hook and line while sea mammals were trapped or harpooned. Clams were dug up on sandy beaches and crabs were caught in traps or speared with sharp sticks at low tide.

Eulachon—The Small Fish with the Big Stink

No discussion about fish in Bella Coola would be complete without mentioning eulachon. This herring-like fish, a member of the smelt family, figures prominently in First Nations culture. Like salmon, it spawns in fresh water and spends the rest of

its life in the ocean. In late March, large schools of eulachon usually spawn along the shoreline of the lower Bella Coola River. Since the 1990s, however, the numbers have fluctuated greatly and in latter years the run has all but disappeared. Eulachon spawn has been noted in the last three years, but the amounts have barely been detectable. Not much is known about the eulachon, and the cause for the rapid decline in the Bella Coola River is something of a mystery. Its demise may be linked to the shrimp fishery, in which eulachon is a discarded bycatch. Or the decline may be the result of changing ocean conditions or interception in other fisheries.

Next to salmon, eulachon, or *sputc*, were of primary importance to the Nuxalk people. During the short period in early spring when the eulachon returned from the sea to spawn, wooden boxes built on the riverbank were filled with wriggling eulachon and left to cure for a few days. In these "stink boxes" the meat would break down, making the oil easier to render. The pungent mass was then boiled with water to release the oil, which was skimmed off the surface—a gruelling, smelly job that usually took a couple of days.

Eulachon oil was highly valued as a condiment, especially as a dip for dried fish, and as a food preservative. But it was also used for medicinal purposes, lamp oil and

Above:
An eulachon spawner arrives back at the Bella Coola River. The once-plentiful eulachon, a traditional staple of the Nuxalkmc, have become extremely scarce in the past five years.

Below:
Chiefs Andy and Anfinn Siwallace by an overgrown and unused eulachon tub.

even as a hair tonic. Because the eulachon, also called a candlefish (a dried eulachon burns like a candle), had so many different uses, it was a key item of trade. Consequently, the main trade routes from the coast through the mountains to the Interior became known as "grease trails."

Scientific analysis has shown eulachon oil to be extremely healthy. According to Dr. Harvey Thommasen, who has studied traditional foods while providing health care to the people in Bella Coola, eulachon grease is "a rich source of vitamin A and omega-3 fatty acids, as well as a good source of calcium, iron and zinc." Nuxalk elder Lillian Siwallace adds that eulachon grease was used to cure constipation, and taken as a warm drink to treat sore throat, pneumonia and cold symptoms. To take advantage of this tonic, though, you have to get past the strong fishy taste of eulachon grease.

Left:
Andy Siwallace tasting eulachon grease at the last run of eulachon on the Bella Coola River in 1998.

Below:
Eulachon in the smoke house.

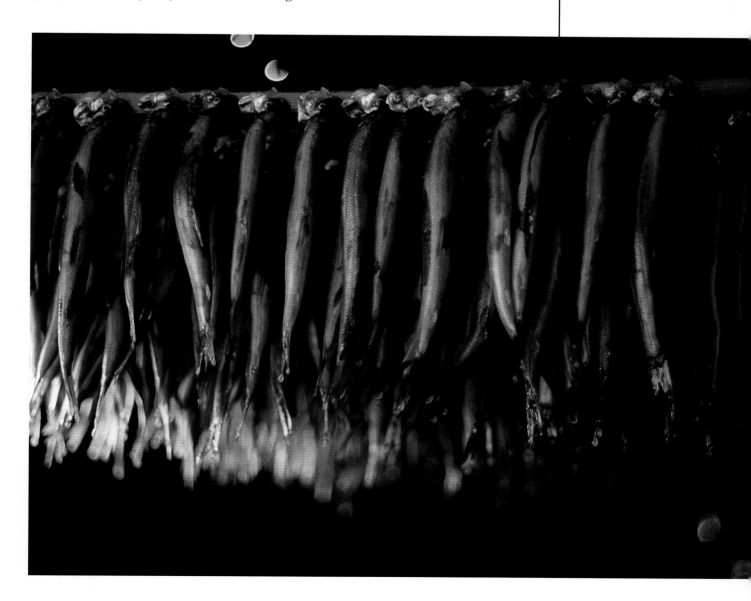

CHAPTER 4

The First Peoples

Previous pages:
The petroglyph beds at
Thorsen Creek near Bella
Coola are some of the
richest in the province.

Above:
An early stone tool used
for chopping.

In pre-contact times, abundant runs of salmon provided a plentiful food supply for the populous and diverse aboriginal communities of the Central Coast. The Nuxalk people of Bella Coola are connected linguistically to the Salishan First Nations, but they are an outlying group, geographically separated from other members of their language family. The neighbouring First Nations belong to different language families, with the Wuikinuxv (Oweekeno) of Rivers Inlet to the south, the Heiltsuk of Bella Bella and the Xaixais (pronounced *hay-hays*) of Klemtu belonging to the Wakashan language family. The Kitasoo, now also located at Klemtu, are of Tsimshian origin. To the east the Ulkatcho people of Anahim Lake are affiliated with an Athabascan language group.

The earliest radiocarbon-dated evidence of human presence on the Central Coast has been uncovered at Namu, where archaeologists have unearthed leaf-shaped points and large-flake stone tools that are more than 10,000 years old. One theory is that they may have been deposited by the first people who came to North America from Asia. Many anthropologists believe these people crossed the Bering Strait about 12,000 years ago and spread south, using a number of different migration routes, one of which was along the West Coast.

Centuries of conflicts and alliances have forged relationships that influence political dealings among Central Coast First Nations today. In many cases, the different nations' territories overlap as a result of territorial wars, historical sharing of resources and intermarriages between the families of different bands. On a personal level, the people get along well and many families from different villages are directly linked with one another. Trade among these communities has been conducted since time immemorial and people routinely get together for potlatch feasts, sporting events and other celebrations.

The Nuxalk People

Originally, Nuxalk families in their tribal groupings occupied areas associated with the major rivers draining into the North and South Bentinck Arms of Burke Channel, Kwatna Inlet and the Dean Channel. Today, the descendants of these families reside in Bella Coola, having relocated here in the late 1800s in order to be close to the trading post and to recover from the devastating effects of the smallpox epidemics. The establishment of the reserve system under the Indian Act also served to concentrate the population of Nuxalk people at the mouth of the Bella Coola River.

Numerous archaeological digs conducted by Dr. Phil Hobler, the former chair of the Archaeology Department at Simon Fraser University, and now a Bella Coola resident, confirm the long-term occupation of various village sites in the Bella Coola valley. At the oldest site, called Tsini Tsini, on a bench above the Talchako River, a large collection of stone chips from an ancient work site has been unearthed. It is estimated

Above:
An ancient culturally modified cedar with healing lobes partially covering the old 'plank' scars.

Left:
SFU archaeological dig at Tsini Tsini. Approximately 9,000 years old, it is the oldest recorded site in the Bella Coola valley.

that the site was in use more than 9,000 years ago. At that time most of the rest of the Bella Coola valley would only recently have emerged from the sea. Ten thousand years ago the ocean extended east into the Bella Coola valley and the shoreline was located above the mouth of the Nusatsum River. These ancient shorelines intrigue archaeologists piecing together patterns of human settlement on the coast. Since most village sites or camps were situated along the shoreline, archaeologists often conduct their studies in seemingly unlikely locations, more than 45 metres (150 feet) above the present sea level.

A village site called Qwliutl near Stuie, in Tweedsmuir Park, was in use about 1,000 years ago while Snxlh, located near the village of Bella Coola on Four Mile Reserve, was in use until 1907. Large villages were also located at Noosgulch (Nusqalts) Creek, Burnt Bridge and several other places.

These sites exhibit the greatest diversity of housing styles on the Central Coast. At Qwliutl examples of shallow pit houses resemble those in the Interior. At Noosgulch, some of the houses were elevated on posts and some were built directly on the ground in the same manner as they were farther downriver at Snxhl.

Villages were usually situated on a terrace above the riverbank or seashore. In 1894 Ted Levelton, a Norwegian settler, described the Bella Coola village as containing "great big old houses. They would be 40 feet wide and probably 100 feet long—terrific big houses." The row of cedar plank longhouses with their elaborately decorated facades facing the water must have been an impressive sight. Several had large totem poles with hollowed-out passages in the base through which guests entered the house.

With large, permanent villages and secure food supplies, the Nuxalkmc developed a rich culture. Each of the ancestral families had their own mythic account of how their first ancestor descended to earth, arriving on one of the surrounding mountaintops. Disguised as birds or animals and supplied with food, tools and knowledge, these ancestors came down the mountains and built villages. To support themselves, they claimed ownership of the surrounding areas. This family history, or *smyusta*, was a sacred text that defined the family lineage. It also established the system of hereditary chiefs with authority over the traditional family territory.

In traditional Nuxalk belief, every activity of human life was governed by the supernatural beings that abound in the surrounding mountains and forests. These spirits were represented in family crests that depicted the bird and animal cloaks that the first ancestors wore as they descended to earth. The raven, bald eagle, grizzly bear, black bear, wolf, whale, black fish, merganser, loon, deer, and the mythical double-headed snake *sisyulh* and fish-like monster *sk'amtsk*, were the crests chosen by the first arrivals, and they figure prominently in Nuxalk art and culture. Carved depictions of these crests were often displayed at the entrance to the family home. The most powerful crest was the raven, or *qwaxw*, which was sent by the Great Spirit to guide and teach the ancestors. A trickster, the raven was the one that stole the sun in order to provide light for the world. And because some of the original people came to earth by sliding down the sun's eyelashes, or rays, the sun is also commonly depicted in Nuxalk art.

Petroglyphs (rock carvings) and pictographs (rock paintings) are widely distributed in Nuxalk territory. Best known are the excellent petroglyphs at Thorsen, or Squmalh, Creek. While not directly datable, the age of the earliest Thorsen Creek petroglyphs can probably be measured in thousands of years. The most recent were made with steel tools, perhaps as recently as the late 19th century.

Our knowledge of the Nuxalkmc has been greatly enriched by Margaret Siwallace, who documented the language and culture of her people. Her contribution to ethnobotany and ethnomedicine leaves an invaluable legacy for the preservation of Nuxalk culture. The significance of Margaret's work earned her an honorary doctorate from the University of British Columbia. Trained for leadership from an early age, she fulfilled that responsibility with grace and rare ability for many years until her death in 1985.

Art Saunders, Silyas, in his studio. A retired logger, Art started carving late in his life and is regarded as one of the most skillful Nuxalk artists.

Bella Coola Meets *Kon-Tiki*

The Norwegian archaeologist and explorer Thor Heyerdahl visited Bella Coola in 1939–40 to study, among other things, the Thorsen Creek petroglyphs. Because of their similarity to Polynesian art forms, Heyerdahl theorized that people from British Columbia, drifting on prevailing currents and winds, originally settled Hawaii. This was before Heyerdahl became famous by sailing the balsa raft *Kon-Tiki* from Peru to the Raroia in the South Pacific to promote his theory that Polynesia was settled from South America, and he was not yet the intrepid figure he became. One of his guides reported that he was afraid of not only bears but also mice. Originally he intended to make only a short stopover, but while he was in Bella Coola the Germans overran Norway, so he became stranded in Canada without means. One of the people who befriended him was Clayton Mack. Heyerdahl wanted to go to Kwatna Inlet to view the fine pictographs there and Mack offered to take him in his gas boat if Heyerdahl would buy the gas, but Heyerdahl was too broke even for that. Mack ended up donating his own gas. Around the coffee pot Heyerdahl asked Mack if he thought his Nuxalk ancestors might have sailed to Hawaii. Mack doubted that they could have made it in dugout canoes, but came up with the idea they might have done it on giant rafts of kelp. Heyerdahl later made an ocean crossing in a craft made of reeds, but stopped short of trying kelp.

Thorsen Creek petroglyph site is both powerful and mystical.

Early Contact

The first documented contact between the Nuxalk people and Europeans was during the summer of 1793 when the explorers George Vancouver and Alexander Mackenzie both penetrated the territory on separate missions. At first, life changed only gradually.

Fur trading in the 1830s and 1840s was the first enterprise to link the Nuxalkmc with European commerce. The pace of change accelerated as contacts increased with traders arriving by sea. The Hudson's Bay Company maintained strict rules against using alcohol in trade but less principled traders commonly used it. The introduction of alcohol further eroded the social fabric of First Nations. Then came the diseases. The smallpox epidemic of 1836 is believed to have claimed about a third of the coastal aboriginal population. A repeat epidemic in 1862 accounted for more than 19,000 deaths. These catastrophic events did more than anything to undermine

The raising of the totem pole in front of Acwsalcta school in 2002. The pole was carved by the students.

traditional First Nations society. The anthropologist Wilson Duff estimated the Bella Coola population at 2,000 in 1835; by 1885 their numbers were down to 450 and by 1929 to 249.

The churches, aware of the social breakdown and believing the solution was to convert coastal peoples to Christianity, began to dispatch missionaries to the region. The first mission in Bella Coola was established by the Methodist Church in 1883 at the invitation of Chief Tom Henry, otherwise known as *Tactalus*. The Reverend William Pierce, a half-Native preacher from Port Simpson, became the first minister to be accepted among the Nuxalkmc.

Through various declarations of the Canadian government, the First Nations' rights to commercial resources were restricted. At the same time, resource extraction licences were granted to settlers in the hope of encouraging development. As whites gained the upper hand they became more aggressive in their dealings with First

The Nuxalk Nine

German tourists who flock to modern Bella Coola hoping to encounter grizzly bears and Native peoples would no doubt be surprised to learn that members of the Nuxalk nation once visited their country over a hundred years ago. It happened this way: in 1885 B.F. Jacobsen, a Norwegian who collected Native artifacts for museums in Europe, decided to cash in on the German mania for things Native by bringing them the real article. Jacobsen persuaded Chief Tom Henry and eight adventurous members of the Bella Coola band to spend a year touring Germany, demonstrating tribal customs. Jacobsen and his unlikely troupe of entertainers, most of whom had never walked on a paved road before, took a steamer to San Francisco, crossed the US by train, caught an ocean liner in New York and arrived in Germany three weeks later. The Nuxalkmc were a big hit, crisscrossing the country doing traditional dances, conducting lectures and hamming it up for German crowds. They returned home the next year, safe and sound and full of remarkable stories.

One of the troubadours, Alec Davis, acquired a steady girlfriend and learned to speak fluent German, a skill he kept all his life. "It is much easier than the Bella Coola language," he said.

"German women followed us around," said Billy Jones, the last surviving member of the Nuxalk Nine. "They wanted to marry us."

One historic impact Bella Coola's wandering minstrels had involved a young museum clerk named Franz Boas. When Boas took in one of the Nuxalk performances, he was so inspired by Chief Tom and the boys that he switched careers and spent the rest of his life studying aboriginal peoples. He later visited Bella Coola in person and wrote the classic text *The Mythology of the Bella Coola Indians*. Boas became one of the world's greatest anthropologists and his enduring interest in peoples of the BC coast caused it to be one of the most studied regions in the aboriginal world.

Nations. In 1877 the government dispatched the Royal Navy warship HMS *Rocket* to the Nuxalk village at Kimsquit to investigate a report that the villagers had seized an American trading ship. Despite the fact that the ship had been nowhere near Kimsquit and no evidence was found in the village, Kimsquit was bombarded and destroyed. The provincial superintendent of Indian Affairs, Dr. Israel Wood Powell, later admitted the attack was "probably" a mistake, but no compensation was offered.

Many First Nations cultural practices, especially the potlatch, were outlawed in 1884. The potlatch was the most important ceremonial activity of coastal First Nations and often involved feasting, dancing, singing and gift giving. The greater the gifts a host could bestow on his guests, the greater his and his tribal group's status would become. Potlatches confirmed the overall social structure of the community.

The potlatch and other ceremonial practices were curtailed or practised in secret until 1951 when the *Indian Act* was finally relaxed. Since then, elders have struggled to revive traditional culture, and since the 1970s in particular, Nuxalk song, dance and artwork have enjoyed a renaissance. "It's sad, though," laments Lillian Siwallace about the lost knowledge of her culture. "It's like our language is now a second language that only a few people speak."

With the coming of the fish canneries in the 1890s and logging in the early 1900s, the Nuxalkmc along with other Central Coast First Nations became day labourers in those enterprises. Today, there are approximately 1,200 Nuxalkmc, of whom about three-quarters live in Bella Coola. Unemployment hovers at the 70-percent level, bringing predictable social problems. The band is governed by an elected chief and council, although the traditional government of hereditary chiefs still plays a strong role in political decision-making.

The Nuxalk people have never surrendered their territorial rights and title and they have so far not participated in the land claims treaty process, which they consider fundamentally flawed. Culturally, the Nuxalkmc are concerned about the potential for exploitation but they also see the need, as Nuxalk cultural teacher Lance Nelson says, "to explain and spread information and knowledge about one of the most sacred areas on earth."

Despite their troubled history, the Nuxalk people are a kind and giving people who welcome visitors with a ready smile and a friendly greeting of "Yaw!" Their outlook was well represented by the late Darren Edgar (Ayamaas), the unofficial, candy-distributing goodwill ambassador of the Nuxalk people, as anyone who had the good fortune of taking his tour of Bella Coola will attest.

Below:
Amanda Siwallace shows there's nothing like salmon prepared the traditional way.

Following pages:
The tiny pastoral settlement of Firvale with Nusatsum Mountain on the left and Salloomt Mountain on the right.

The First Peoples

CHAPTER 5

The Europeans Come to Stay

Above:
Eagle on derelict boat.

Below:
Table Top Mountain with
the Bella Coola River in
the foreground.

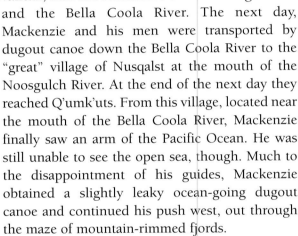

Bella Coola occupies a special place in the annals of North American exploration, for it was here that the fur trader and explorer Alexander Mackenzie reached the Pacific in 1793, and at age 29 became the first person known to have crossed the middle part of North America.

Near what is now the western edge of Tweedsmuir Provincial Park, Mackenzie caught a first glimpse of the Bella Coola valley and its "stupendous" mountains. From there, the trail descended quickly to the valley, where he was immediately welcomed into the "friendly" Nuxalk village Nulleax, near the confluence of Burnt Bridge Creek and the Bella Coola River. The next day, Mackenzie and his men were transported by dugout canoe down the Bella Coola River to the "great" village of Nusqalst at the mouth of the Noosgulch River. At the end of the next day they reached Q'umk'uts. From this village, located near the mouth of the Bella Coola River, Mackenzie finally saw an arm of the Pacific Ocean. He was still unable to see the open sea, though. Much to the disappointment of his guides, Mackenzie obtained a slightly leaky ocean-going dugout canoe and continued his push west, out through the maze of mountain-rimmed fjords.

Three days later, Mackenzie found himself facing increasingly hostile remonstrances by some Heiltsuk men. He was unable to determine the cause of the trouble, but noted the men repeating a word that sounded like "Macubah." What Mackenzie didn't know was that Captain George Vancouver had passed through the Bella Coola area on his coast-wide charting expedition only six weeks previously, and had apparently left some locals with a bad impression of white explorers. Reluctantly, near Elcho Harbour in Dean Channel, Mackenzie gave up his drive to the open ocean. It was at this western limit that Mackenzie mixed some vermilion in bear grease, found a flat rock and laboriously spelled out one of the great understatements of exploration: "Alex Mackenzie from Canada, by land, 22nd July, 1793." A monument now stands at Elcho Harbour directly above

Alexander Mackenzie Heritage Trail: A Continental First

Established in 1985, the Alexander Mackenzie Trail is the first heritage trail in British Columbia and retraces part of the route followed by the explorer Alexander Mackenzie as he in turn followed well-established First Nations trading routes or grease trails. The trail begins at the confluence of the Fraser and Blackwater Rivers between Prince George and Quesnel, then follows a series of forest roads, wagon roads, footpaths, rivers and coastal waterways to Sir Alexander Mackenzie Provincial Park on Dean Channel. The main part of the trail crosses the undulating terrain of the Fraser Plateau before dropping down the eastern edge of the Coast Mountains at Burnt Bridge in the Bella Coola valley. Here the trail takes to the river, although most people use Highway 20 to reach Bella Coola, about 50 kilometres (30 miles) to the west. From Bella Coola, a boat can be hired to complete the journey to Mackenzie Rock in Dean Channel. Standing at the site where Mackenzie reluctantly gave up his quest for the open Pacific, you can still sense how vulnerable the explorers must have felt, dwarfed by the overpowering landscape on one hand and threatened by discontented aboriginal residents on the other.

The trail that traverses Tweedsmuir Park covers nearly 420 kilometres (260 miles) of rough terrain and takes at least 18 days to complete. The most scenic section of the trail is the 80-kilometre (50-mile) stretch within Tweedsmuir Park, a trek of five to seven days. To take part in the Mackenzie experience, you needn't complete the whole trail in one push. It can be tackled in different sections. The eastern part of the trail passes ranches and fishing lodges; fly-in arrangements can be made for drop-off and pickup. Still, hikers must be able to backpack for at least a week. The trail is also a popular route for extended pack-horse rides.

Prospective hikers should be aware that the western part of the trail through Tweedsmuir is very remote and help is not readily available. In the open alpine areas it is easy to lose your way, especially in bad weather, so one should be familiar with map and compass. It is best to travel in groups of three or more, and to notify the RCMP of your departure and expected return dates. Plan your hike for late summer or early fall—any earlier, and you'll get eaten alive by blackflies and mosquitoes, especially in low, damp areas. For more information, check out *In the Steps of Alexander Mackenzie*, published by the Alexander Mackenzie Trail Association, Box 425, Kelowna BC, V1Y 7P1.

Sir Alexander Mackenzie rock in the Dean Channel, where the explorer ended his westward journey to the Pacific.

the spot where these famous words were daubed on the shoreline rock. Mackenzie retraced his journey to Fort Fork on the Peace River, where he arrived only a month later.

The publication of his *Voyages from Montreal* in 1801 earned Mackenzie celebrity status and sparked US President Thomas Jefferson to commission the Lewis and Clark expedition, which in 1805 became the second overland party to reach the Pacific.

Fur Trade, Gold Rush, Missionaries and Settlers

The explorations of Mackenzie and Vancouver put to rest the notion of a navigable Northwest Passage through North America to the rich lands of the Orient, and attention turned to the exploitation and development of the newly discovered territory. What followed was the gradual influx of fur traders and fortune seekers.

In 1805–6, Mackenzie's firm, the North West Company, established four trading posts in the Central Interior and began moving furs (mostly beaver) east across the country using overland canoe brigades. After the NWC merged with the Hudson's Bay Company in 1821, the combined company decided to get to the region increasingly by sea and built a series of forts along the coast, servicing them with trading vessels including the pioneer steamships SS *Beaver* and SS *Otter*. With the burgeoning sea traffic up and down the coast and the east–west trade through the inlets, Bella Bella on Campbell Island must have seemed ideally situated as a coastal transportation hub, linking the Bella Coola, Owikeno and Dean watershed corridors to the ships plying the coast. In 1833 the Hudson's Bay Company chose it for the site of the first major trading post on the Central Coast, Fort McLoughlin. An imposing structure was erected, but the results were disappointing. It closed after ten years and HBC trading vessels filled in as mobile trading posts, venturing up Burke Channel to Bella Coola.

First Nations were the main suppliers of fur and, as experienced negotiators with their own internal trade, many profited. Many also acted as guides for the occasional party of Europeans who journeyed east from Bella Coola to trade for furs and explore the Interior, first by dugout "spoon" canoes up the Bella Coola River and then by foot up the grease trails. Traffic surged in 1860 when the Cariboo gold rush started and miners began accessing the goldfields through Bella Coola. In the Interior, First Nations had to endure an invasion of gold-seeking newcomers and the 1862 smallpox epidemic at the same time. Animosity erupted into the Chilcotin War in April 1864, when the Tsilhqot'in (Chilcotin) attacked and killed 14 workers who were

Spoon canoes were the main mode of transportation in the Bella Coola valley prior to the coming of the Norwegian settlers and the construction of a wagon road up the valley. Carved from a single cedar log, the canoes were manoeuvred upriver mainly by using cedar poles.

cutting a road from Bute Inlet to the goldfields under the leadership of Alfred Waddington. To capture those responsible for the insurrection, the fledgling colony of British Columbia immediately dispatched the 51-gun frigate HMS *Sutlej*, the *Beaver* and the supply ship *Labouchere* with 510 officers and men. Overnight, the sleepy backwater of Bella Coola was beset by an influx of Europeans whose numbers, for the first time, rivalled those of the First Nations. During that tense summer, five more white men were killed. In early fall, the Tsilhqot'in agreed to negotiate terms of peace and sent a party of representatives to meet government officials at Quesnel, but instead of negotiating, the government hanged them. It was not until 1999 that the BC government formally apologized for the hangings at a ceremony in Quesnel.

In any case, the episode halted all road building, and the notion of a wagon road through the Chilcotin was abandoned when a route up the Fraser Canyon was completed in 1865. In the summer of 1867, the Hudson's Bay Company established a small trading post next to Q'umk'uts at the mouth of the Bella Coola River. As the only authority in the hinterlands, the Hudson's Bay Company ended up with the responsibility of maintaining peace between settlers and the First Nations populations. During this time, unrest among the First Nations continued and most Europeans began to move out of the area. In 1882 the Hudson's Bay post at Q'umk'uts was sold to John Clayton, who had served as postmaster there in 1875 and 1876. He went on to become the leading non-Native entrepreneur in Bella Coola and Bella Bella during the late 19th century. Clayton's store was located on the south side of the Bella Coola River, near what is today the Bella Coola Motel. The Nuxalk villages were also located on the south side of the river and their canoes continued to be a major means of transporting goods and people on the Bella Coola River.

Clearing the heavy riverbottom forest took backbreaking hand work by the first settlers, who worked without the aid of oxen, horses or machines.

Norwegians—Clearing the Land

Early European settlement in the Bella Coola area had been limited to a handful of people attached to trading ventures or missions, but thanks to an unlikely chain of events, that was about to change dramatically. One of the traders who passed through Bella Coola during the 1880s was the tireless Norwegian art collector B.F. Jacobsen, a multi-faceted man who was to play a key role in Bella Coola history as a pioneer and entrepreneur, among other things. When a local chief urged Jacobsen to bring settlers into the valley in order to create business and employment opportunities, Jacobsen obligingly put the word out, mainly to other Norwegians.

One interested party was that of a Lutheran pastor in Minnesota's Red River Valley, the Reverend Christian Saugstad. A pocket of disaffected Norwegians living in the Red River Valley at that time had come to America from the cold and forbidding fjords of northern Norway, where for centuries their ancestors had struggled to eke out a living. They were prepared to struggle even harder to forge a toehold in the new world. Instead they found themselves deposited upon a fertile, open prairie fated to become one of the most productive grain-growing regions in the world, although at that time it was suffering from the same economic depression that was plaguing the rest of North America. The Norwegians were disheartened, but not only because of the low crop prices. They missed the comforting backdrop of enclosing mountains and the moderating presence of the ocean. The Reverend Saugstad and his followers held strict views that put them at odds with others in their congregation and they longed for a new location that would be "suitable for a pious and virtuous life free from outside influences." The Bella Coola valley, with its great isolation and fjord-like setting, seemed made to order.

This is how it came to be that on October 30, 1894, the sidewheel steamer *Princess Louisa* pulled up in front of Bella Coola and began unloading 84 Norwegian men,

The compound of early Bella Coola entrepreneur John Clayton, formerly a Hudson's Bay Co. trading post.

women and children into Nuxalk dugouts. The first group was followed in May 1895 by a second numbering about 60 (mostly wives and children of the first group). In November another group of about 60 Norwegian immigrants arrived from the midwestern states, bringing the total to about 200. The task of establishing a white settlement in the valley was at that time almost impossibly daunting, but through a twist of fate Bella Coola had been provided with a group of settlers who possessed not only the life skills to survive the extreme hardship they were about to face, but also the determination. It was truly a match made in heaven.

After their initial disappointment at the density of the forest and the amount of drudgery that lay ahead, the industrious Norwegian farmers set to work clearing land, building cabins, digging gardens and taming the wilderness. They proved very hardy and gave the new white community a solid core from which to grow. Their main settlement formed around Hagen B. Christensen's store 19 km (12 miles) up the valley and became known as Hagensborg. The picturesque Augsburg Lutheran church was built there in 1904, and though it was taken over by the United Church in 1949, it remains a focal point of Norwegian heritage.

Milo Fougner, son of the Norwegian colonist Iver Fougner, who was the first teacher in Bella Coola and the Indian agent in the early 1900s, attributes the perseverance of the Hagensborg settlement to the women:

"This Mrs. Hansen in particular, her husband was one of the first to get discouraged, and just after New Year's he said, 'Well, we're going back to Minnesota.' 'No,' she said, 'I've seen the fall here now in Bella Coola and part of the winter, and I want to see what the spring is like.' So when the spring came, he said, 'Well, now we can get back to Minnesota just in time to plant crops.' 'Well,' she said, 'I've seen the winter now and the spring is so beautiful, I'd like to see the summer.' And that was it. They stayed. They're both buried here."

It is doubtful that the settlers would have succeeded without the help of the Nuxalkmc, whose dugouts provided much of the transportation up and down the river. Norwegian pioneer Annie Levelton recalled those early days when the two communities worked closely together. "The Indians were surprisingly very good to us. They could have resented us pretty badly but they were awfully good to us. And we were good to them."

When the colonists arrived, the main Nuxalk village was on the south bank of the river near the present reserve. The store and trading post operated by pioneer trader John Clayton was in the same area. In 1904 another white village was laid out on the north side of the river where there was more winter sunshine, and eventually the Nuxalk village picked up stakes and followed its white neighbours to the sunny side. It turned out that site was a flood plain and in 1924, after constant dousing by the Necleetsconnay River, the white village shifted back across to the gloomy but dry side of the river. The Nuxalkmc held out but after severe flooding followed the whites back in 1936, ending up on the shady side where they had started out. Today, Native and non-Native Bella Coola continue side by side, divided by a common road and separate cultures.

The Bella Coola eulachon run provided the Nuxalk with a major trade item in earlier times. Though the great eulachon runs are now just a memory, the river remains the lifeblood of the valley.

Farming, Fishing and Forestry

Many of the descendants of the original Norwegian settlers are living in the valley today and 10 "century farms" are still in the same family name after more than 100 years. The relatively wide and flat Bella Coola valley, with pockets of rich alluvial soils, a warm summer and a long growing season, proved to be one of the few places on the Central Coast where commercial farming is possible. By the early 1900s Bella Coola was a main supplier of fruits and vegetables to people up and down the Central Coast. During the 1920s the government even operated an experimental research farm in the valley. Some of the original fruit trees can still be seen on the property at the end of Grant Road. At least 12 different heritage varieties of apples with such delectably exotic names as Winter Banana and Prapple can be found in the valley's private orchards.

Agriculture remained a viable business until refrigerated transport barges began to bring food from Vancouver. The demise of neighbouring resource communities such as Ocean Falls and the various cannery villages also reduced demand for produce. Today, most fields in the valley are used to grow hay for beef cattle, for the many recreational horses and even for a few llamas. With a heritage of self-sufficiency, almost every household has a vegetable garden and in such a fertile setting it is hard not to become a hobby farmer.

Tom Draney, whose cousin Robert built the successful Namu cannery, partnered with John Clayton to build a cannery at Bella Coola in 1900. Tom soon discovered that he did not have his cousin's stomach for fish, often becoming violently sick at the sight of the slimy cargo being offloaded from the boats. The partnership dissolved after only two years. BC Packers bought the operation and ran it until 1935, when it

Opposite:
The Augsburg Church, once the pride of Bella Coola's Lutheran pioneers, stands in the village of Hagensborg.

Below:
The Hammer farm property in Hagensborg.

Opposite:
Hooktender attaching a
choker on a cold deck log
pile in the landing.

Below:
A salmon gill net hangs
on net racks at the Bella
Coola wharf in readiness
for the season's opening.

was turned into a net loft, which is still the dominant landmark in the Bella Coola harbour. Across the harbour, the picturesque remains of the Tallheo cannery are an inviting place for the curious to explore. Built in 1917 by the Bella Coola pioneer and entrepreneur B.F. Jacobsen, it closed in 1947 but continued to operate as a store and gas bar for fishing boats until 1978. The site is now being restored bit by bit as a quaint, seasonally operated lodge and restaurant. To reach the cannery, guests are treated to some living history as they zip across the inlet aboard *Ye Old Lady Bug*, a rum-runner from the Prohibition era.

If farming was the Bella Coola settlers' first choice of livelihoods, fishing was probably second, but in the end the leading economic engine of the community and the whole region turned out to be the forest industry. At first, logging on the Central Coast was conducted primarily to supply local construction. Bella Coola's first mill, built in 1898, provided the lumber for the dock on the north side of the inlet, adjacent to the original townsite. With the coming of pulp mills at Swanson Bay (1909) and Ocean Falls (1912), huge timber leases were granted throughout the coast and in the Bella Coola valley. Handloggers used boats to tight-line logs into the water and also floated them down the major rivers. Later, steam donkeys and A-frames, erected on large rafts, were used to pull the hand-felled timber down to the water from high up on the hillsides overlooking the inlets. The logs were then boomed up into rafts and towed to Ocean Falls. Much of the coast was logged this way between 1910 and 1940.

As technology improved, and the easily reached shoreline timber was harvested, the loggers began moving farther inland. In 1917 a rail line was built along the Kimsquit River and a steam locomotive hauled logs down the valley to be dumped into the estuary. This railway was moved to Green Bay on the Nooseseck River just west of Bella Coola in the 1920s, and finally to Kwatna Inlet in 1928. Remnants of the old rail lines can still be found in these valleys.

Jim Sirois

Jim Sirois, grandson of Doc Gildersleve, recounts his years growing up on a logging float camp in *Afloat in Time* (Skookum Press, 1998). One of Jim's stories involves a close call in 1948, when he, Gildersleve and Torkelson were watching the steam-donkey engineer fight a hang-up. A turn of logs attached to the skyline had gotten stuck behind some stumps, with dramatic consequences:

"The skyline tail hold stump at the back end, 1,800 feet away and up the side of the hill, gave way. The entire skyline system and carriage crashed to the ground with a screaming snarl of whipping, slashing and coiling steel cable. Suddenly, the air above our heads was filled with the slicing steel tentacles of a descending skyline cable gone mad, flailing about in giant circles and coiling itself at tremendous velocity and power into a monstrous spring aimed right where the men were standing.

Seeing the danger at the last moment, Andy grabbed Jim and Doc in his bear-like embrace and tumbled them all face-first into the dirt just as the cable cracked above them like a cannon. In another split second they would have been decapitated."

In order to move the giant logs from high up on the hillsides down to the rail sites, high-lead logging systems were used. To rig the high-lead system, cables were hung from tall and sturdy spar trees and logs were suspended to the mainline with chokers, like clothes on a washing line. The winches that were used to pull the logs to the landing were originally powered by steam donkeys. These were the glory days of logging when local legends such as Doc Gildersleve, Andy Torkelson and Jack Allison earned their "bull of the woods" reputations.

Railway logging gave way to truck logging in the 1930s and 1940s and the spar trees were replaced by diesel-powered steel "yarders" in the late 1940s. Today, mobile yarders with mechanical grapples bring logs to the roadside and more and more,

Ken Zielke conducting a post-logging audit of a cutblock reserve.

helicopters are used to pluck felled logs from the hillsides and drop them in the ocean or at roadside landings. Technological innovation continues but some handloggers still try to scratch out a living along the Central Coast.

It was not until the 1930s that the first "outside" logging company set up business in the valley. The Viking Timber Company promptly went belly up, leaving debts and an unpaid payroll. Some of the employees joined together to form the Northern Co-operative Timber and Mills Association, which evolved into Northcop Logging, then into Little Valley Forest Products, which is currently the only significant industrial wood processing facility on the Central Coast.

After the pulp mill at Ocean Falls wound down in the 1970s, most logs harvested in the area were barged to Vancouver Island and the Lower Mainland. Together with the shipment of fish to canneries farther south, this leaves the Central Coast in the position of being a mere extraction zone once again, much to the dismay of locals, who see their jobs being exported. By the turn of the century a variety of global influences pushed the coastal forest industry into a period of severe economic decline and in 2001, the largest local employer, Interfor, closed its operation in Bella Coola. In 2003 the Ministry of Forests responded by downsizing its local office.

Selective heli-logging in Burke Channel. The cedar logs from this 'show' are towed to Bella Coola where they are processed by Little Valley Forest Products.

Near the top of 'The Hill,' a dramatic descent into the Bella Coola valley awaits.

Conquering the Hill with the Freedom Road

The broad, gently inclined Bella Coola valley offers a ready-made corridor through the formidable barrier of coast mountains that almost everywhere else walls off western Canada from the Pacific, but this advantage has not been as important in local history as one might expect. Alexander Mackenzie got the Bella Coola route to the sea onto the national map before any of the alternate corridors, and it was always considered when succeeding generations sought to develop transportation links between the ocean and the Interior, but for 150 years it kept losing out to competing routes, first to the south, then to the north. At the outset of the Cariboo gold rush in 1859, a detachment of British army sappers known as the Royal Engineers actually started surveying a wagon road in Mackenzie's footsteps, making good use of First Nations grease trails, but the project was abandoned in favour of the Fraser Canyon route. Bella Coola got onto the provincial transport agenda again during the planning of the Canadian Pacific Railway, but was again passed over for the Fraser Canyon. Next up was the Grand Trunk Pacific Railway, and when that went north to the Skeena River corridor in 1914, it began to look as if Bella Coola's overland connection to the Interior, so strongly suggested by nature, would never get built by man.

During the Second World War, the army took a strategic interest in the matter and managed to bulldoze a road through the upper valley to the foot of the Chilcotin escarpment, but settled for merely upgrading the telegraph line from there to 150 Mile House. After the war, exasperated valley residents took matters into their own hands. With next to no money, a group of stubborn men and women set about finding a route for a road out of the valley, then commandeered a couple of bulldozers and began gouging away at the Chilcotin escarpment from both sides. With a clank that still resounds, the two machines touched blades on September 26, 1953. A year's work by 10 paid employees and countless volunteers had produced 77 kilometres (48 miles) of new road at a cost of $62,000.

The construction of the so-called "Freedom Road" was an epic accomplishment, one that has graduated into Bella Coolan legend. Tourists can still get a vivid sense

Above:
The Freedom Highway's famous 'Hill.'

Left:
The last switchback on Bella Coola's infamous hill, leaving just one more steep incline to negotiate before reaching the valley floor.

of what the feisty pioneer builders faced by following Highway 20 from Williams Lake to Bella Coola. From the mile-high edge of the plateau at Heckman Pass, the most extreme stretch of public highway in British Columbia drops down the Hill at an 18-percent grade. Even though the road has a harrowing reputation, there have

Commercial troller plying the seas in Fitz Hugh Sound.

been relatively few serious accidents on it—probably because every driver is paying full attention when white-knuckling down this steep, narrow dirt road with its sheer drop-offs. In 2003 the narrowest stretch of the Hill got a 50th-anniversary upgrade when a precipitous rock face was blasted away.

CHAPTER 6

Bella Coola Country Today

Previous pages:
The lower end of the
Bella Coola valley facing
west to Bella Coola town-
site and North Bentinck
Arm.

Above:
The landmark Kopas
Store in Bella Coola.

Below:
Jeanette McCauley at the
calf-roping event.

Opposite above:
Erik and Annika Granander
captivated by the rodeo.

Opposite below:
View of Bella Coola
townsite.

As you fly from Vancouver north to Bella Coola, the signs of civilization quickly vanish below. In minutes the maze of roads and roofs has been replaced by the Coast Mountains' sea of white peaks. After an hour of peering out at countless and mostly nameless pinnacles and glaciers, you descend into impossibly narrow valleys. Looking up, not down, at the passing peaks, you may well wonder where a plane can touch down in this jagged landscape. But a few sharp, mountain-dodging turns later, you enter an incongruously lush valley dotted with farmhouses and, to every passenger's relief, an airstrip. Once on the tarmac, surrounded by steep granite cliffs and distant mountaintops, you can feel your senses sharpening, your inner clock slowing and your stresses evaporating.

If the sun is blazing and the streets are bustling, it must be the Canada Day weekend at the beginning of July, when the Bella Coola valley Ridge Riders put on an old-time rodeo, the biggest party in the valley. Forget the groomed glitz of larger stampedes—this is family fun with a spirited edge. Start with feisty horses and ornery bulls, add some dust and corn on the cob, throw in some wild cow milking, cow patty bingo and "ladies undecorating," mix it all up with beer and cardiac burgers and finish it off with a two-step twirl with a sparkling cowgirl, and you'll understand

why ranch hands from all over the Chilcotin and beyond flock to Bella Coola in July.

Occasionally a rodeo rider lands badly, breaking or spraining something. Fortunately, there is a surprisingly well-equipped hospital at hand. In an age of government cuts Bella Coola has maintained a basic level of medical care with strong support from the United Church. The hospital is a source of local pride, attracting such notable country practitioners as Dr. Alistair Anderson, Dr. Nancy Anderson, Dr. Harvey Thommasen and Dr. Ray McIlwain, Director of the United Church's Health Services in British Columbia. Other services and amenities in Bella Coola are basic rural fare: retail stores, a credit union, library, seniors' home, government administration, elementary and secondary schools and an airport with daily service to Vancouver. The *Coast Mountain News* reports on the local happenings every two weeks, but in between issues, locals keep up by tapping the rainforest telegraph at the Bella Coola Valley Restaurant or at the Bay Motor Hotel coffee shop, where local scuttlebutt travels fast. Here conversation is less about politics and fashion and more about the condition of the Bella Coola River—is it up or down, are the fish in or out, is it clear or silty? Or: what is the state of the Freedom Highway—is it smooth or rough, is it slippery or dry?

During basketball season the Nuxalk Hall is packed each night of the week with fans cheering on their favourite teams. This arena is also used for large potlatch celebrations. A few kilometres up the valley, the Fall Fair Grounds are home to a country fair and logger sports on the Labour Day

weekend. Also on these grounds is Lobelco Hall, the usual venue for major celebrations, dances and the local theatre guild's twice-yearly productions. In Hagensborg a small outdoor pool is open in the summer and an equally weather-dependent outdoor skating rink opens for a few cold weeks in winter. The Bella Coola Valley Art Centre in Hagensborg next to Sir Alexander Mackenzie Secondary School displays and sells works by local artists during the summer. Native artwork such as prints, masks, wood carvings and jewellery can be found at Kopas Store. A number of Nuxalk artists are also opening up their own studios to display and sell their work (inquire at the Nuxalk Administration Office for directions). The Bella Coola Museum displays artifacts and other historical items in a heritage cabin on Highway 20 in downtown Bella Coola. Another interesting museum is the Norwegian Heritage House, situated in an old cabin on the highway in Hagensborg. Run by the Sons of Norway, it depicts the life of the original Norwegian settlers.

Apart from the rodeo and fall-fair whoop-ups, the valley is a quiet place, but that doesn't mean there's nothing doing. It's just that Bella Coola is an undeveloped spot suited to self-reliant people, and this applies to guests as well. Although tourist services are steadily increasing with guided fishing trips and nature tours, river rafting and drift-boating, traditional and cultural tours and local art workshops, visitors to the valley must rely on their own initiative to get the most out of what the area has to offer.

Opposite:
Nuxalk culture is part of the curriculum at Acwsalcta or "place of learning."

Below:
Rene Morton, daughter of Bella Coola pioneer Cliff Kopas, in the Bella Coola Museum.

Bella Coola

The saying "getting there is half the fun" could have been coined just for Bella Coola. Arriving by air affords spectacular views, but to really understand the scale of the place, nothing beats coming in by car, either overland or by ferry. For a number of summers past and hopefully for many to come (check before setting out), BC Ferries has operated a twice-weekly "Discovery Coast Passage" between Port Hardy and Bella Coola, which is more like a mini-cruise than a routine ferry ride. You can either sail direct or enjoy optional stops at McLoughlin Bay (Bella Bella), Shearwater, Klemtu and Ocean Falls. Make reservations well in advance because this popular service is often sold out at the peak of the June–September season. Reserving accommodation in Bella Coola is also recommended. There is a hotel and a motel (with campground) in Bella Coola, another motel in Hagensborg, a famous lodge at Tweedsmuir Park and a growing number of B&Bs, but the choice locations fill up fast.

A popular circle road trip includes stops on Vancouver Island, then north on the ferry to Bella Coola, then east across the Chilcotin along Highway 20, and south again to Vancouver. Awaiting you in the valley is a recreational banquet to suit any age, budget, fitness level and schedule. The region is world-famous for salmon fishing and, at the Dean River, steelhead fishing, but there are plenty of attractions that don't require a rod and reel. Logging roads along the various tributary valleys offer stunning scenery and opportunities to see and photograph wildlife, but they are often in various stages of temporary "deactivation," so check with the local forest ministry field office for up-to-date access information. These roads are ideal for mountain biking, but be sure to pack bear spray, as it's all too easy for two-wheelers to surprise ornery bruins. There are many places to hike, but few trails are maintained and hikers often have to pick their own routes to areas of interest. But that's one of the charms of the Central Coast: you're free to go where you want. A fuller listing of recreational opportunities follows in "A Recreational Paradise."

Above:
Renowned artist Alvin Mack, in his workshop carving a scale model design for a traditional longhouse.

Below:
Bella Coola wharf in the foreground with the old Tallheo cannery across the channel.

Neighbouring Communities

Bella Coola may seem like a lonely spot on the map, but despite—or perhaps because of—the long distances to neighbouring settlements, Central Coast communities share a certain kinship in the struggle to survive and prosper. They are closely linked by history, trade and family connections and rivalries.

Bella Bella

Home of the Heiltsuk First Nation, Bella Bella is situated on Campbell Island, 96 kilometres (60 miles) due west of Bella Coola. Halfway between Prince Rupert and Port Hardy, it is a natural stopover for boats plying the coast. The Hudson's Bay Company fort established there in 1833 prompted Heiltsuk people to relocate to the area from outlying villages, but it operated for only 10 years. In 1868 the HBC reopened a store. "Old Town" continued to grow and by the 1890s the site was too small. The community was moved three kilometres (two miles) north to its present site.

Today, approximately 1,200 mostly Heiltsuk people live in Bella Bella, also known as *Waglisla*. Extremely proud of their heritage, the Heiltsuk maintain a cultural centre that boasts an impressive collection of documents and information about Central Coast aboriginal history and culture. The centre is housed next to the distinctively designed school, which resembles an eagle with outstretched wings when viewed from the air. Other amenities include a hospital, marina, band administration services, a general store, convenience stores, restaurants and a fish hatchery. Visitors can choose from numerous bed-and-breakfast hostels around town, where guests are treated to home-cooked delights, usually caught fresh from the sea.

The Bella Bella school eagle watches over the new school yard playground.

Above:
The boat harbour in Bella Bella.

Below:
Young Heiltsuk dancers performing the canoe dance.

A transportation hub, Bella Bella is situated at a strategic crossroads of the Inside Passage, through which gargantuan cruise ships must squeeze on their way to Alaska. During the summer cruising season, these impressive white ships look oddly out of place in an area where fishing boats and barges are the norm. The booming loudspeakers onboard these floating cities can easily be heard on shore, and when it is announced that "the tiny village of Bella Bella can be seen off the port bow," it is debatable who is more amazed, the passengers on the cocktail deck or the people pausing in their daily routines to gaze at the passing spectacle. The waiting room in the Bella Bella airport is often standing-room-only during summer months as loggers, commercial and sport fishermen change planes en route to coast logging and fishing camps. Year-round ferry service connects the village to Port Hardy.

Across Lama Passage from Bella Bella is the small settlement of Shearwater, established in 1938 as an Air Force base. During the Second World War it was one of five flying-boat stations along the West Coast; one hangar still stands. Developed by local entrepreneur Andy Widsten in 1947 as a marine resort and supply centre, Shearwater also has a great pub and restaurant, the Fishermen's Bar and Grill. It is definitely the place to be during the hectic herring and sport-fishing seasons. Isolated though it is, you can drive there by taking BC Ferries' Discovery Coast route in summer and the Inside Passage service in winter.

Klemtu and Princess Royal Island

At Trout Bay on Swindle Island, 56 kilometres (35 miles) north of Bella Bella, is the isolated village of Klemtu. Nestled behind Cone Island in Finlayson Channel, Klemtu is home to the Kitasoo and Xaixais people. Originally settled in the 1870s to supply wood to fuel steamers plying the coast, Klemtu has evolved mainly as a fishing community. A salmon cannery was in operation here from 1927 to 1968 and, with a population of a little more than 300 people, Klemtu is now striving to diversify its economy through fish farming, logging and tourism. The largest employer is the band-owned fish processing plant, where up to 70 people work. The village has two parts: one on the north side of the bay and one on the south. These two neighbourhoods were once linked by one of the longest wooden boardwalks in the world, on which pedestrians had to hug the railing whenever a vehicle passed. This charming but dilapidated wooden causeway was recently replaced with a very short paved two-lane road that is nevertheless connected to the BC highways system via BC Ferries' year-round service to Port Hardy.

In late summer and early fall, Trout Bay teems with shiny coho and the not-so-shiny chum salmon that are preparing to enter their natal streams to spawn. Schools of flashing fish can be seen racing around the small bay. Hardly a second goes by without at least one "lunker" (up-coast argot for jumper) leaping high into the air. This makes for great sport and, as soon as school is out for the day, kids head to the docks armed with their favourite fishing rods. The parade of smiling children struggling home under the weight of trophy-size salmon is a memorable sight.

The abundance of salmon returning to the doorstep of the community doesn't happen by chance. In a remarkable example of gentle intervention, the Kitasoo practise "ocean ranching," releasing hatchery fry into the local streams in numbers greater than the streams could produce naturally. When the fully grown salmon return after a few years of feeding in the boundless ocean "ranch," they are easily

Klemtu with its new long-house overseeing the entrance to Trout Bay.

Kitasoo and Xaixais drummers and singers practicing inside the longhouse.

caught as they mill about at the mouth of their home stream. This simple and efficient means of managing salmon has been rigidly limited by Fisheries and Oceans Canada, but it is now being tried in other areas.

The Kitasoo and Xaixais have also launched a successful fish-farming business, but there is widespread resistance outside the community. Debate centres on the risk to the marine environment and wild fish stocks. Opposition among those who support commercial fishing is sharpened by the fact that farmed fish drive down the price for wild fish. On the plus side, fishing pressures on wild stocks could be reduced. Coastal communities threatened with economic collapse must carefully weigh the risks and benefits of any opportunity.

The recently completed longhouse at the entrance to Trout Bay is the cultural centrepiece of Klemtu and another symbol of the reinvigoration of a First Nations people. The Kitasoo and Xaixais have also produced a land-management plan that protects more than 40 percent of their territory while acknowledging that some development is necessary to sustain their community.

A key component of the land-use plan is the creation of Spirit Bear Protection Area, 90,622 hectares (223,926 acres) on Princess Royal Island north of Klemtu along the Inside Passage. Princess Royal Island was the lightning rod of environmental controversy on the coast during the 1990s due to its population of white kermode bears. The island and surrounding area are thought to contain 100 to 200 white kermodes, the largest concentration anywhere.

The Central Coast Framework Agreement is, among other things, a first step toward the protection of the kermode bear's temperate rainforest habitat. The Kitasoo and Xaixais will be co-managing the protection area on Princess Royal Island with the province of British Columbia and have established a community-owned and -operated tourism venture, Klemtu Tourism Ltd. (www.klemtutourism.com) to develop ecotourism opportunities. The venture offers "sea kayak and motorboat eco-tours [that] combine the best elements of wildlife, culture and wilderness in the heart of the Great Bear Rainforest." Kayak rentals and motorboat charters are offered, along with full marina services for pleasure craft. The village has two stores, accommodation in a unique floating motel as well as a chain of wilderness cabins and B&Bs in the village.

Rivers Inlet and Oweekeno village

South of Bella Coola, halfway to Port Hardy, is Rivers Inlet. Renowned for its record-sized spring salmon, Rivers Inlet is the home of the Wuikinuxv people, who live along the Wannock River, which drains the silty waters of Owikeno Lake, largest on the Central Coast. This lake once supported one of the largest sockeye salmon runs in British Columbia, but has declined so severely it has been closed to commercial fishing for many years. One of the first major canneries in the Central Coast was the Wadhams cannery at Rivers Inlet. Established in 1887 by Edmund Wadhams, an American gold rush pioneer who originally came to British Columbia in 1858 to seek his fortune on the Fraser River, the Wadhams cannery became one of the longest-lived canneries on the Central Coast. In the fishery's heyday, a fleet of more than 1,000 boats supplied Owikeno Lake and Long Lake sockeye to 22 canneries operating in Rivers Inlet and neighbouring Smith Inlet.

Fishing was carried out mostly at night, when the linen nets were not visible to the fish. The spectacle of those nights was "wondrous and magical," recalls Glenn MacKay, a retired fisherman and local history buff. "The whole fleet was scattered throughout the inlet with all their cabin and net lanterns bobbing in the dark." The Wadhams cannery finally closed in about 1941 but the buildings and wharf were still in place in 2003 and the site was operated as a fly-in wilderness resort called Wadhams Outpost Adventures. The rise of commercial sport fishing has helped to make up for the demise of commercial fishing. Recently the Wuikinuxv have acquired cutting rights in the local forest, which will hopefully provide some economic relief.

Home to the Wuikinuxv people of Rivers Inlet, Oweekeno village is located halfway up the Wannock River with Owikeno Lake in the background.

Oweekeno village has been the central settlement for the Wuikinuxv since the early 1900s. Today, about 100 people live there; another 350 or so band members live outside the territory. Even though their heritage has a powerful homeward pull, it has taken great determination for the Wuikinuxv to keep their community viable. This determination was seldom more evident than in the case of the migrating schoolhouse. After years of lobbying with Indian Affairs, a schoolhouse was built on the outskirts of the village along the shores of the Wannock River. Unfortunately, the shoreline is a travel corridor for grizzly bears and children faced real danger as they made their way to and from school. After repeated requests to move the schoolhouse to the village centre, in 1975 the residents picked up the school and moved it themselves. "You should have seen the look on the face of the Indian Affairs Agent the next time he flew in," says Chief Frank Johnson, "seeing the school in the middle of the village!" Such is life in the hinterland. You have to be able to take matters into your own hands.

Yakze, a totem pole, belonging to Johnny Johnson, is located in the Oweekeno village.

Namu

Another notable settlement on the Central Coast is Namu. Located near the mouth of Burke Channel on the east shore of Fitz Hugh Sound, Namu is situated opposite the Hakai Provincial Recreation Area, the largest marine park on the West Coast. It is a popular stopover for boaters plying the Inside Passage. Namu is a largely vacant group of buildings left over from its heyday as a cannery; only a few residents remain. But Namu has a much longer and more significant history. Radiocarbon dating has confirmed human presence here more than 10,000 years ago, making it one of the longest continuously occupied sites in Canada.

In Heiltsuk language, Namu means "place of high wind or whirlwind," and when Robert Draney built the cannery there in 1893, he respectfully retained the First Nations name, christening it the Namu Canning Company Ltd. The family business flourished and in 1909 a mill was built on the site to provide lumber for the construction of more buildings and crates for the cans. Draney sold the cannery in 1912 and over the ensuing years it changed ownership many times, finally ending up under the control of BC Packers in 1928. The last operating cannery on the Central Coast, Namu was finally closed in 1970. Today, no large-production canneries are left in the region, although some First Nations have initiated processing ventures where seafoods are cleaned and frozen for transport to market. Of these, the most successful are operated by the Heiltsuk in Bella Bella and the Kitasoo and Xaixais people in Klemtu.

Swanson Bay and Ocean Falls

Two pulp mill towns, one totally abandoned and the other almost, bear witness to the boom-and-bust history of resource extraction in British Columbia. Swanson Bay, on Graham Reach in the Inside Passage, was the site of British Columbia's first pulp mill. Built in 1909, the settlement had a population of 500 in its heyday, but the mill closed in the mid-1920s. The settlement was eventually abandoned during the Second World War and is now virtually overgrown by the rain forest from which it sprang.

Ocean Falls was substantially larger and longer-lived than Swanson Bay, but it eventually met the same fate. Once a thriving community of 5,000 people with one of the largest hotels north of San Francisco, Ocean Falls is now a virtual ghost town. Ocean Falls Company Ltd. began clearing land for the town in 1906, a sawmill was completed in 1909 and in 1912 the pulp mill was ready for production. In 1915 the company name was changed to Pacific Mills Ltd., which Crown Zellerbach Canada Ltd. bought in 1954. Reportedly the rainiest town in Canada, with annual precipitation of 4,368 millimetres (172 inches), Ocean Falls may seem an odd spot to have established a complex industrial facility. But all that rain pouring into Link Lake made the location ideal for the cheap hydroelectric generation all pulp mills require and a first-rate deep-sea port combined to overcome the disadvantages of the remote, sodden site.

For an isolated community, it had a surprisingly high level of services and community infrastructure: a theatre, dance hall, gym, library, giant hotel and well-stocked stores. The mill was breaking production records and life was good. The full-sized swimming pool was the training ground for a swim team that became world-famous. Among its most distinguished members were the Olympic swimmers Sandy Gilchrist and Ralph Hutton, holder of 32 Canadian records, winner of a silver medal in the 1968 Olympics and later a member of the International Swimming Hall of Fame.

In the 1960s Ocean Falls started to go downhill. The pilings supporting the mill were found to be inadequate for the new high-speed paper machines taking over the industry. The mill could no longer compete and closed in 1973. The government of the day tried to revive the operation by purchasing the mill, but the timber rights remained in Crown Zellerbach's hands. In 1980 the mill closed permanently. Twenty years later, only about 40 or 50 people lived in Ocean Falls and most of its buildings had been removed or demolished. The rain, however, continues to fall and the hydro-electric plant continues to operate, supplying power to the island communities of Shearwater and Bella Bella.

Remnants of the old pulp mill at Swanson Bay being overtaken by the rain forest from which it sprang.

Tweedsmuir Park

Sprawling over 981,000 hectares (2.4 million acres) between Anahim Lake and Bella Coola is Tweedsmuir Park, British Columbia's largest provincial park. Nearly 225 kilometres (140 miles) from north to south, it is a vast wilderness virtually unchanged since Baron Tweedsmuir of Elsfield, the 15th governor general of Canada, explored the area by float plane and packhorse in 1937. Lord Tweedsmuir declared in 1938, when the park was established, "I have travelled over most of Canada and have seen many wonderful things, but I have seen nothing more beautiful and more wonderful than the great park which British Columbia has done me the honour to call by my name." Today, visitors can catch a glimpse of what Lord Tweedsmuir was referring to from Highway 20, which bisects the park's southern half, but the main attractions can only be reached by the same methods available to His Lordship—float plane, hoof or foot—although snowmobiling is allowed in a designated area in winter.

The park marks a dramatic change in topography where the broad Interior plateau meets the towering barricade of the Coast Mountains. The ecology is primarily alpine tundra and subalpine forest, where meandering meadows produce a dazzling display of alpine flowers that attract visitors from around the world. Woodland caribou inhabit the plateau areas and grizzly bears roam the Atnarko and Dean River valleys. Other attractions include the aptly named Rainbow Mountains, which display the volcanic history of the area in brightly coloured bands of acid-stained, oxidized rock. Another favourite destination is the Turner Lake chain, where backpackers can rent canoes to explore the picturesque lakes with the ragged Coast Mountain skyline as a backdrop. This lake chain drains into the Atnarko valley at Hunlen Falls, one of Canada's highest, with a vertical drop of 253 metres (830 feet).

Following page:
Hunlen Falls hangs frozen over the Chilcotin escarpment in early spring.

Below:
A view near the western boundary of Tweedsmuir Park in the Bella Coola valley with Mt. Stupendous in the background and the Gyllenspetz pioneer cabin in the foreground.

Tweedsmuir Lodge (Stuie)

Overlooking the Atnarko River with its world-class salmon fishing is Tweedsmuir Lodge, built by the famed outdoorsman Tommy Walker in 1929 as a gentlemen's hunting and fishing retreat. Before being renamed in honour of Governor General Lord Tweedsmuir, it was known as Stuie ("a pleasing place of repose" or "a quiet place"), after the old First Nations village there.

From its earliest days, Tweedsmuir Lodge's combination of isolation and comfort attracted a steady procession of distinguished visitors. Lord Mountbatten's daughter, the Countess Mountbatten of Burma, spent a few days at the lodge. One of the more memorable guests was Sir Edmund Hillary, of Mount Everest fame. Hillary stayed at the lodge in 1986 while testing outdoor equipment in the mountains surrounding Bella Coola. Today, guests can make arrangements to stay in the rustic "Hillary" cabin.

Above:
A view to the south from Tweedsmuir Lodge.

Below:
Picturesque Tweedsmuir Lodge.

The original Tweedsmuir Lodge built by Tommy Walker burned down in 1950.

The lodge was bought in the 1940s by a Second World War veteran and banker, Lieutenant-Colonel Gordon Corbould, after his wife heard at a bridge game that it was for sale. The Corbould family fell in love with the lodge, only to be devastated in May 1950, when it burned to the ground. In a characteristic display of rural neighbourliness, valley residents rushed to the aid of the homeless family and the lodge was rebuilt in time to receive guests for the fall fishing season. The lodge remained in the Corbould family until 1995.

Anahim Lake

With an area population of about 1,000, Anahim Lake is Bella Coola's closest neighbour to the east, and the two communities have long been linked, first by the grease trails and later by the construction of the Freedom Road. The most westerly community in the Chilcotin, Anahim Lake has a definite "Interior" character. Here, the dry climate and grassland landscape are a world away from the cloud-shrouded mountains and islands of the Central Coast. The rhythm of life in Anahim Lake is controlled more by the spring "breakup" and haying seasons than by tides and salmon.

One of the last communities in the Chilcotin to be settled, Anahim Lake was named after the Tsilhqot'in leader Chief Anaham. Following the Chilcotin War in 1864, Anaham and his people were relocated east to the Anaham reserve in the Chilcotin River valley. To avoid confusion between the two places, the first postmaster, Stan Dowling, changed the spelling of the settlement to Anahim Lake, but locals still pronounce it Ana-HAM. Dowling is also credited with the 1938 launch of the

Saviour of the Swans

Lonesome Lake, part of the Atnarko River system, is where the legendary pioneer Ralph Edwards carved out a home in the wilderness in 1912.

Edwards was inducted into the Order of Canada in 1972 for his conservancy work in feeding the starving trumpeter swans through some unusually hard winters at Lonesome Lake. In 1932, Edwards arranged with the Canadian Wildlife Service to provide funds to buy barley, horse-packing and flying in about 4,500 kilograms (10,000 pounds) of the grain into the lake annually. Edwards' gallant intervention saved this subpopulation of trumpeter swans from certain doom. The Lonesome Lake population of 100 swans at one time represented about one-third of the estimated remaining population wintering between southeastern Alaska and the Columbia River. But Richard W. McKelvey, wildlife biologist for the Canadian Wildlife Service, reports that the big birds have recently increased so dramatically that some 6,000 Alaskan trumpeters now winter on or near the Pacific coast. A number of books have been written about Edwards' independent and inspiring life, including his own account as told to Ed Gould, *Ralph Edwards of Lonesome Lake* (Ulverscroft, 1979, 1997).

Ralph's sister-in-law Isabel Edwards, a city girl born in England and raised in Victoria, was equally remarkable. Isabel and her husband Earle spent one winter with Ralph in the Coast Mountains—to help her husband's asthma—and found themselves still there 50 years later. Her trials and tribulations are amusingly documented in *Ruffles on My Longjohns* (Hancock House, 1997).

Anahim Lake lies on the eastern side of the Coast Mountains. Great trout fishing, family recreation and dynamic vistas draw many repeat visitors.

legendary Anahim Lake Stampede, held every year on the weekend following the July long weekend. Along with the Bella Coola rodeo and the world famous Williams Lake Stampede, both held on the preceding July long weekend, this is the place where real cowboys and cowgirls whoop it up.

Since the 1930s, Anahim Lake has mainly been supported by ranching, guide outfitting and trapping. In the 1900s, the Ulkatcho people gathered in the area so that their children could attend school. Economic growth has been driven by forestry in

Anahim Lake Resort nestles amid the trees as evening settles over the lake.

recent decades, in particular by the establishment of the Carrier Lumber mill in the 1980s. In the early 1990s, the operation was closed in a controversial decision by the provincial Ministry of Forests. From the ashes of this controversy, West Chilcotin Forest Products Ltd. emerged in 1994 as a successful partnership between the Ulkatcho First Nation, the Anahim community and Carrier Lumber. Anahim Lake is working to diversify its economy; its many trophy fishing lakes, lodges and an expanding arts community are seen as key opportunities for the future.

CHAPTER 7

A Recreational Paradise

Previous pages:
There is no end to
challenging terrain for
skillful heli-skiers.

Above:
Overlooking Glacier Lake.

The Bella Coola country offers some of the most spectacular outdoor adventure in North America, but the best of it is quite challenging and unless you are an experienced outdoors person, this area is probably best approached with the assistance of one of the many guides, outfitters or tour operators serving the area. These can be researched through travel agencies specializing in eco-travel or by contacting Bella Coola Valley Tourism (www.bellacoola.ca). At the same time, there is much in the region that can be enjoyed by an average family, and this section includes a brief listing of some better-known sites and activities, both easy and difficult. For further research, Scott Whittemore's *The Bella Coola Valley and Vicinity: Hiking Trails & Routes* has detailed descriptions of the more popular places and many adventure tourism services maintain informative web sites.

Tweedsmuir Park

Rainbow Range Trail: This trail takes hikers into the brightly coloured Rainbow Mountains, also known as the Painted Mountains, from Highway 20 at the East Branch Creek parking lot just west of Heckman Pass (top of the Hill). Allow at least three days to enjoy this trip thoroughly. After meandering through Engelmann spruce and subalpine fir forest, the trail gradually climbs to open alpine tundra. Bring a good map and compass, as it is easy to get lost in the open tundra when fog rolls in. The summer flowers are spectacular. Bugs can be a problem in early summer, but start to die off in the latter part of August. Keep a lookout for caribou and bears.

Atnarko tote road: This small road leaves Highway 20 at the bottom of the Hill and heads east up the Atnarko valley for about 13 kilometres (eight miles) to the Hotnarko River parking lot. This road crawls along the Atnarko River, offering serene views of riffles and pools teeming with salmon during late summer on one side, and tumbledown remnants of old homesteads on the other. The road also cuts through some very rough scree slopes, which only 4x4 vehicles with high ground clearance and good tires should attempt to cross. This is heavy-use grizzly territory, so beware. Allow an hour in and an hour out.

Stillwater and Hunlen Falls: From the Atnarko tote road parking lot, hikers can continue to Stillwater Lake, about an hour's walk along a moderately difficult trail that crosses some dry, bouldered talus slopes and snakes along the lush valley bottom. Pack bear spray and make noise as you walk through this grizzly bear corridor. Stillwater is the first of a series of lakes in the upper Atnarko and is extremely rich fish-rearing habitat. No fishing allowed.

Hunlen Falls: At Stillwater the trail to Hunlen Falls branches off and leads immediately to a steep climb—with 78 switchbacks—of 600 metres (2,000 feet). It is about 13 kilometres (eight miles) to Turner Lake and the viewpoint overlooking Hunlen Falls. Fit hikers can make it in and out in a day, but it is wiser to camp overnight. If you want to spend a few more days in the area, you can rent canoes to paddle the Turner Lake chain.

Belarko Spawning Channel to Fisheries Pool: This stretch of the Atnarko River is popular for fishing, and on hot summer days it is also great for inner-tubing. Start at either the parking lot by the Belarko Spawning Channel or at Tweedsmuir Lodge, and lazily float down to the Fisheries Pool picnic ground. It is best to travel in groups to minimize encounters with bears. The Fisheries Pool is also great for swimming and snorkelling among migrating salmon. Beware of innocuous-looking but deadly log-jams, where currents can easily sweep people (or dogs chasing sticks) to a watery grave.

Talchako Forest Service Road: This logging road leaves Highway 20 near the western edge of Tweedsmuir Park, crosses the Bella Coola River and heads southeast along the Talchako River, one of the main tributaries of the Bella Coola and a principal source of the silt that gives the Bella Coola its distinct milky colour. The road goes for approximately 30 kilometres (19 miles) to Gyllenspetz Creek; along the way it crosses a number of slide areas that can deposit gravel and rocks on the road, barring access. The road affords striking views of mountains, waterfalls and the turquoise

Above:
This grizzly has grown fat on the plentiful salmon of the Atnarko River, improving its chances of surviving winter hibernation.

Opposite below:
A side channel of the Atnarko River in autumn. Though much smaller than the Fraser and Skeena Rivers, the Atnarko ranks third in coast salmon production.

river. Grizzly bears can be seen on the road, especially where it runs close to the river. We recommend a 4x4 but two-wheel-drive is possible for at least the first part.

Burnt Bridge Trail lookout: At the western edge of Tweedsmuir Park, a 15-minute walk will take you to a lookout with another panoramic view to the west of the upper Bella Coola valley. Park at the Burnt Bridge picnic ground. (This is also near the junction of the Alexander Mackenzie Heritage Trail and Highway 20.)

From Tweedsmuir Park to Hagensborg

Mountain goats: The cliffs immediately above the tiny settlement of Firvale provide one of the best opportunities to see mountain goats up close, especially in early spring and late fall. The goats will also come down to these low elevations in the summer due to a number of salt licks in the area and can sometimes be seen right at the roadside.

Capoose Summer Trail: Approximately halfway between Firvale and the Canoe Crossing highway bridge, the Summer Trail snakes up the mountains on the north side of the valley. Unmaintained, it's really more a route than a trail, and it is hard to find. But it will lead fit hikers to the top of the ridge, and panoramic views of the jagged peaks south of the valley, Thunder Mountain to the north and the Bella Coola valley itself. A long day of hiking will take you to Fish Lake in Tweedsmuir Park, which was an important historical junction for a number of trade routes.

Noosgulch forest service road: This logging road leaves Highway 20 on the north side of the Canoe Crossing bridge and quickly climbs up into the Noosgulch valley and heads north toward imposing Thunder Mountain (2,625 metres/8,750 feet). A 4x4 is recommended but two-wheel-drive is possible.

Glacier Creek or Cacoohtin forest road: To access this 4x4 logging road, take Hammer Road turnoff on the south side of the Canoe Crossing bridge and drive past the homesteads picturesquely located by the Bella Coola River. The forest service road heads south toward 2,627-metre (8,756-foot) Defiance Mountain, with its dramatic glacier churning down from the base of the sheer summit wall. A short bushwhack and creek crossing near the end of the road will put you into the open to scramble up the scree slopes on the west side of the steep-walled valley to the toe of the glacier. Allow a full day to enjoy the area.

Medby Rock lookout: A fire lookout used to be situated at Medby Rock and as such offers excellent views of the Bella Coola and Salloomt valleys. Follow the signs leaving Highway 20 immediately on the east side of the Nusatsum River bridge. The trail climbs up through second growth and into a stand of old-growth Douglas fir until you reach the rocky outcrop at the lookout. Remnants of the old telephone wire can still be seen strung along some of the trees. This is a moderately difficult half-day hike.

Nusatsum forest service road: A two-wheel-drive vehicle can negotiate this logging road, one of the main attractions in the valley. The road will take you approximately 25 kilometres (15 miles) up the Nusatsum valley to the awesome Odegaard falls viewpoint and trail (about 45 minutes through mountain hemlock forest to the base of the falls) and up into the subalpine pass leading to the Noeick valley. The pass is absolutely stunning, with towering mountains and a variety of avalanche chutes, meadows, ponds and scrubby alpine forest. Grizzly bears use this area periodically but mountain goats can usually be spotted on the south-facing cliffs. The Ape Lake trail also starts from this road, approximately three kilometres (two miles) beyond the Odegaard falls parking lot. Due to winter avalanche activity, driveable access

Opposite:
When the glacial melt ceases by late autumn, the waters of Clayton Falls diminish, revealing its sculpted granite bed.

beyond the falls parking lot may or may not be possible, but it is easy walking or mountain biking nine kilometres (5 1/2 miles) to the lookout opposite the imposing Mount Purgatory and the Noeick River valley. This was the site of an interesting natural phenomenon in 1984 and 1986 when glacial dams at Ape Lake collapsed, releasing torrents of water known as "jokulhlaups" that scoured the Noeick valley, destroying stands of timber, logging-road bridges and salmon spawning grounds.

Short walks

Salloomt forest trail: Easy meandering trail through old-growth and second-growth timber along the Bella Coola River. Located on the north side of the river near the confluence of the Salloomt River. Cross the Bella Coola River at the Bailey bridge and follow the Salloomt road to the well-marked parking area.

Walker Island: This regional district park invites one to wander among Sitka spruce, cottonwood and heritage cedar trees, some showing ancient scars where Natives removed planks. There are a number of sloughs and ponds bearing signs of beaver activity.

Lower Valley and Bella Coola

Thorsen Creek petroglyphs: One of the richest concentrations of petroglyphs on the coast. This site has great significance to First Nations, so you will be showing respect—and learning more—if you go with a guide. Check with the Nuxalk Nation Administration Office or tourism outlets to arrange a guided tour.

Bella Coola estuary: Birds and unique plants abound on the estuary and visitors are free to roam the area, but beware of rising tides that can cut off your return route. The area is also excellent for canoeing or kayaking—but don't get caught on the far side of the inlet when the afternoon westerly starts blowing on sunny days, which can be as miserable for paddlers as it is delightful for windsurfers. Surprisingly, North Bentinck has conditions rivalling those in Howe Sound and Nimpkish Lake, but very few windsurfers know of the secret. Launch from the Clayton Falls creek picnic site two kilometres (1 1/4 miles) west of the Bella Coola harbour.

Clayton Falls viewpoint and picnic site: This is a scenic spot with numerous picnic tables, next to the ocean looking toward the Talheo Cannery. Across the road is a short trail leading behind the hydro generating station to a viewpoint overlooking Clayton Falls. This is a great place to cool off on a hot summer day, but stay behind the fence. The smooth-walled canyon with its stepped falls has dangerous currents and whirlpools.

Clayton Falls forest service road: This 4x4 road takes you over a 1,280-metre (4,200-foot) ridge overlooking South Bentinck Arm, with excellent views of the Coast Mountains' jagged peaks. There are short hikes into Mount Gurr Lake, a crystalline alpine emerald; Bentinck Arm lookout and Blue Jay Lake campground and picnic area. The latter half of this road has been deactivated with many cross-ditches so a high-clearance vehicle is necessary.

Larso Bay big cedar tree: This is an impressive, gnarly old giant—it takes 15 Grade 6 students to reach around the base—left behind when the area was logged in the early 1900s. The bay can be reached only by boat; the tree is a 15-minute walk up the logging road.

Air tours: For an unforgettable experience, charter a plane with Bella Coola Air or a helicopter with West Coast Helicopters and take an aerial tour of the spectacular surroundings, or get dropped off for some remote hiking or camping.

Drift fishing for
spring salmon on
the Atnarko River in
Tweedsmuir Park.

River fishing, drift-boating and rafting: A number of guides take fishermen or sightseers down the river on specially designed drift-boats. Rafting is also available.

Canoeing: It is possible to canoe the Bella Coola River, but this should be attempted only by experienced paddlers. There are tricky currents and dangerous log-jams.

Nature tours: Guide and outfitter Leonard Ellis operates heli-access grizzly bear viewing on the Kimsquit River, which has one of the densest populations of grizzly bears. Gary Shelton also offers interpretive nature tours of the Bella Coola valley.

Skiing: Heli-skiing is a recent arrival, with Bella Coola Helisports flying skiers to some of the largest verticals in North America (2,100 metres/7,000 feet). The local ski club also runs a small rope tow at East Branch near the top of the Hill in Tweedsmuir Park on weekends.

Snowmobiling: East Branch in Tweedsmuir Park is renowned for the excellent snowmobiling terrain and snow conditions. Closer to Bella Coola, the upper Clayton Falls area is gaining popularity among snowmobilers for its varied terrain and rugged mountain scenery.

Kayaking: The Central Coast is quickly gaining a reputation as a kayaking mecca, especially the maze-like outer coast region around Hakai Recreation Area and the islands around Bella Bella and Princess Royal Island. BC Ferries is helping to increase the popularity of this activity by providing "wet launches" from the Discovery Coast Ferry. Ecotourism operations offering kayaking are taking hold in Bella Bella and Klemtu, but so far there are few established campsites and paddlers must be self-sufficient. The best campsites often have high heritage value for the local First Nations, so treat the area respectfully and practise good kayaking and camping etiquette.

Steelhead fishing: The Dean River, north of Bella Coola, is world-renowned for its summer steelhead run. From July to the end of September, discriminating fishermen are whisked from the Bella Coola airport by helicopter or small plane to one of the four fishing lodges operating on the Dean. Using jet boats, expert guides give fortunate anglers a memorable experience of great fishing, wildlife viewing and relaxation.

In addition to locally based operations, a growing number of outside tour operators have started to serve the tremendous upsurge of interest in the Central Coast by offering packaged sailing tours out of Port Hardy, Victoria and Vancouver. They can be reached through adventure travel agents or through such web sites as www.small-shipcruises.com.

Conclusion

When the prospect of moving to Bella Coola presented itself, I did not really know where it was and I had no idea how quickly the place would set its hook in me. The original plan was to stay for five years, tops, but after 13 years we are more entrenched than ever. What is it about Bella Coola that makes it so hard to leave?

Today, the spirit of life in Bella Coola is strongly influenced by its geography, remoteness and history. It is a coastal community, even though it lies more than 120 km (70 miles) inland from the open sea. It is a pastoral farming community located more than 450 km (280 miles) away from the nearest stoplight. It is a community of ancient families who have lived here since time immemorial and it is a community of newcomers with ties to distant parts of the world.

Development in Bella Coola has been slow by western standards and the community still retains a pioneering character that is dominated by the cycles of nature. Here daily life is entwined with the natural world. Whether a guide drift-boats customers down the river, a logger yards timber off the hillside, a fisher untangles salmon from a net, a rancher inspects the hay crop, a biologist studies a bear sow with cubs, a mushroom picker scans the forest floor, a heli-skier shreds deep powder or a retailer gives fishing advice, all are intricately connected to the surrounding environment. Here you feel like you are part of something. Here you only need to step out the door in order to go for a "walk in the park."

Here is a place that still feels wild. Even though all the comforts of modern life are available, a pioneering, self-reliant spirit still prevails. And even though you can shield yourself from nature's forces, you still feel vulnerable. This is a humbling feeling that connects you to your surroundings—you become more aware of nature, more in tune with the subtle changes of the seasons. Walled in by imposing mountains and at the end of the road, you can't help feeling isolated, but this only intensifies the Bella Coola valley's strong sense of community. Here nobody is anonymous.

Through my work I have experienced the Central Coast as few others do. Whether from the air, on the ground or in a boat, I have seen the area in all its vast complexity. As a forester I have had the satisfaction of working in the outdoors and experiencing the daily drama of life in this wondrous rain forest. I have had the privilege of developing friendships with individuals who trace their families' habitation of this land back thousands of years, and with so many in all walks of life who embody the Bella Coola spirit.

As it has so many times in the past, that spirit is once again being tested by change. The long decline of the forestry and fishing industries has been paralleled by steady depopulation of the region, marked by the virtual disappearance of important local communities like Ocean Falls and Namu. Bella Coola also finds itself in a phase of contraction, and some sceptics fear it may eventually follow its neighbours into oblivion. Others believe this will never happen, given the valley community's unique advantages—its central location, its livable spaces, its appealing climate, its Freedom Road and the irrepressible spirit that built it.

Chief Anfinn Siwallace of the Nuxalk Nation personifies this optimism in saying: "People think we are at the end of the road, but in fact, Bella Coola is really at the beginning of a new road." This "new road" leads to a region that contains world-

Soaring into the future.

renowned natural wonders whose survival is secured through the extraordinary conservation measures of recent years. Protected areas have been doubled and a fifth of the Central Coast area, amounting to more than one million hectares (2.47 million acres), is now under protection status. Management of natural resources is being guided by conservation principles to provide a sustainable economic base, and together these measures would seem to assure that Bella Coola will continue to be at the centre of one of the world's great wild and natural spaces for centuries to come.

—Hans Granander

Photographer's Note

It was in the spring of 1984 that I first came to Bella Coola. For the previous 11 years I had lived in the Cariboo town of Wells, where the snow begins to fall as early as September and ice remains on the lake as late as mid-May. It's a land where winter rules. As I slowly made my way down the mountain pass into the Bella Coola valley and the coastal rain forest revealed itself to me, I realized I had found a very special place. Two decades later this lush, generous and gentle world still captivates me.

Here I've been able to do the things I've wanted to do, and photography has become a means to reveal the wonders I discover almost daily. Whether catching brood stock for our local salmon hatchery, assessing and restoring streams or simply exploring on my own, cameras have always been with me.

My first photographic exploration involved the salmon species in our area. I began with their fresh-water food supply, the insects, and after five years of intensive collecting, identifying and photographing, I had a reasonably good idea of the life forms inhabiting our lakes and streams. As with any path of discovery, mine diverged, intersected and converged with others. Over the years I've tried to explore as many of these paths as I could and began to see for myself the amazing interconnectedness of landscape and life forms. Invariably, all paths consistently led back to the salmon: from the insects that sustain them in their youth to the eagles, bears, humans and others that rely on their flesh, to the riparian plant communities that flourish from their nourishing carcasses, I could not have asked for a better guide to the complexities of the Central Coast.

I've had the freedom and opportunity to explore and document the varied landscapes of this complex part of the world, where mountain and ocean influence all. I have learned that through photography, I can reveal the beauty of the life forms bound to these influences.

When Hans Granander approached me nearly two years ago to contribute to this book, I immediately understood that this could be my chance to share my vision of a land that continues to thrill me. Thanks, Hans, for this opportunity and for your enthusiasm.

—Michael Wigle

Acknowledgements

This book would not have been possible without the help and support of many people with first-hand knowledge of the environment, history and life in Bella Coola and the Central Coast, and Mike and I are eternally grateful to all those who donated their time and expertise to this project. In particular, I am very thankful to the following, who patiently tolerated my pestering, helped to review portions of the manuscript and provided advice on how to correct the various iterations: Rene Morton, Eva and Harvey Mack, Lillian and Andy Siwallace, Tracey Gillespie, Russ Hilland, Sandie MacLaurin, Dr. Phil Hobler, Neil O'Borne, Jennifer Carpenter, Ken Dunsworth, Wilfred Humchitt, Gary Shelton, Grant Scott, Frank Johnson, Larry Greba, Lance Nelson, Laurie Vaughan, Linda Price, Evelyn Edgar, Steven James, Bert Struik and Ken Corbould. We are also indebted to Anfinn Siwallace, Alvin Mack, Patricia McKim, Glenn MacKay, Bob Lenci, June Vosburgh, Larry Jorgenson, Betty Sangster, Cassidy Sill, Duane Pedersen, William Schlackl, Bella Coola Valley Trail and Nature Club, Terry and Keith Corbould, Gary Runka and Harvey Thommasen for providing specific first-hand information, as well as their perspectives on the current state of affairs. To fill in the gaps in the photo portfolio, the following people graciously let us use some of their excellent images: Keith Pootlass, Patrick Armstrong, Jai Condon, Dave Chamberlain, Evan Loveless, Ray Pillman, Duane Pederson, Dr. Phil Hobler and Clark Hans for contributing the graphic prints. In addition, thanks are due to Wayne Sissons of Bella Coola Air, Lorna Schneider of the Bella Coola Museum, John Morton of Kopas Store, Peter Tamaryn of Tweedsmuir Lodge and especially Richard LaPointe of West Coast Helicopters for believing in the project and persuading others to follow.

Mike and I would also like to thank the staff at Harbour Publishing: Shane McCune, Shyla Seller and especially Vici Johnstone, Ann-Marie Metten and Roger Handling for their tireless push to get this book out. Finally, I thank my wife Caroline, daughter Annika and son Erik for their support in allowing me to indulge this dream and their patience with me for the countless chores I did not do and the fishing trips that I missed while I was plunking away at the keyboard.

We are deeply indebted to you all in helping us realize our vision of putting together a book that captures the essence of Bella Coola and the Central Coast.

A heartfelt thank you to all,

Hans and Mike

Second printing, 2006

Published by
Harbour Publishing Co. Ltd., P.O. Box 219, Madeira Park, BC V0N 2H0
www.harbourpublishing.com

Cover and page design by Roger Handling
Maps by Roger Handling

Photographs by Michael Wigle except when otherwise noted below.
Photographs by Hans Granander on pages 8, 9, 10 (above), 11, 13, 20, 26, 28, 31, 32, 35, 36, 38 (below), 40 (above), 50 (above), 51 (below), 59 (above) 94 (below), 95 (below), 102, 108, 110 (below), 111, 120, 121, 122, 123 (above), 124, 128, 129, 130, 131, 132, 133, 134, 135, 136, 138, 143 (below), 150 (top), 155; by Jia Condon, 1, 33, 148; by Keith Pootlass, 95 (above), 107; by Caroline Granander, 104; by Heather Conn, 78; by Evan Loveless, 14; by Dave Chamberlain, 93; by Patrick Armstrong, 119, 140; by Dr. Phil Hobler, 98, 99 (below); from the Corbould Family 144; from the BC Central Coast Archive, 101, 112, 113, 114, 115.

Printed in China

Harbour Publishing acknowledges financial support from the Government of Canada through the Book Publishing Industry Development Program and the Canada Council for the Arts; and from the Province of British Columbia through the British Columbia Arts Council and the Book Publisher's Tax Credit through the Ministry of Provincial Revenue.

National Library of Canada Cataloguing in Publication Data

Granander, Hans, 1961–
  Bella Coola : life in the heart of the coast mountains / Hans Granander, Michael Wigle.

Includes bibliographical references and index.
ISBN 1-55017-305-7

  1. Bella Coola River Region (B.C.) I. Wigle, Michael, 1948– II. Title.
FC3845.B44G72 2003   971.1'1   C2003-911165-2

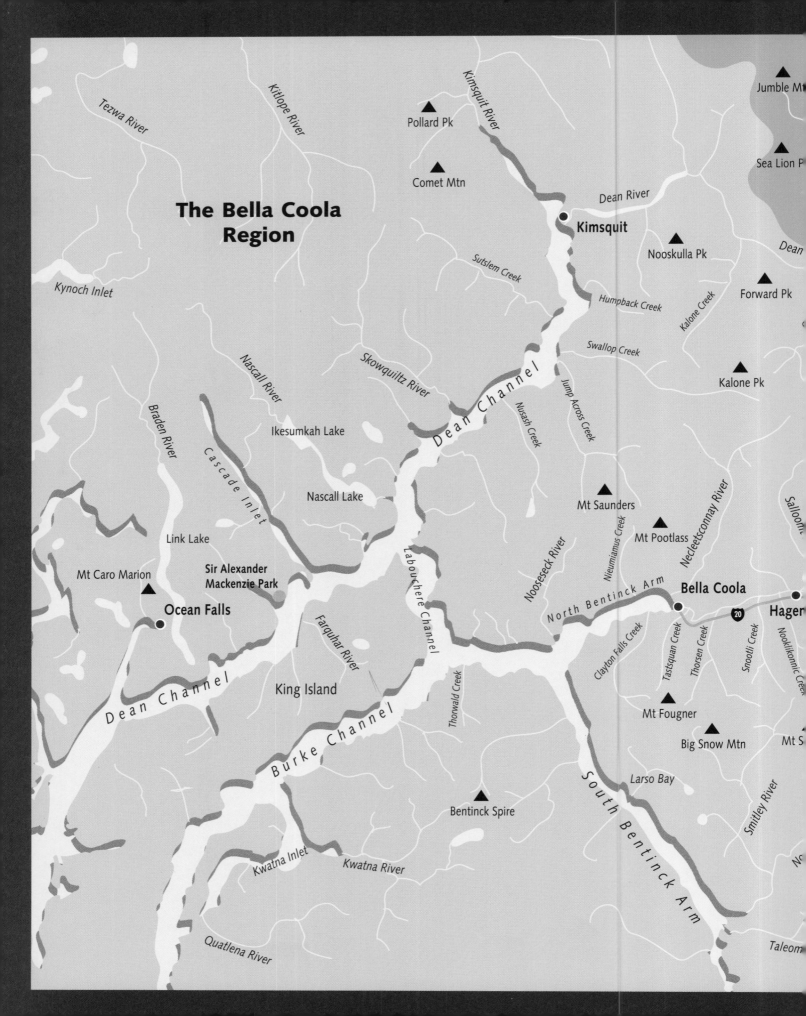

The Bella Coola Region

Tezwa River

Kitlope River

Kynoch Inlet

▲ Pollard Pk

Kimsquit River

▲ Comet Mtn

Dean River

● **Kimsquit**

Jumble Mt ▲

Sea Lion P ▲

▲ Nooskulla Pk

Dean

Sutslem Creek

Humpback Creek

Kalone Creek

▲ Forward Pk

Nascall River

Skowquiltz River

Dean Channel

Swallop Creek

▲ Kalone Pk

Ikesumkah Lake

Nusash Creek

Jump Across Creek

Braden River

Cascade Inlet

Nascall Lake

▲ Mt Saunders

Link Lake

Nooseseck River

Nieumiamus Creek

Necleetsconnay River

Salloon

Mt Caro Marion ▲

Sir Alexander Mackenzie Park

Labouchere Channel

▲ Mt Pootlass

Ocean Falls ●

Farquhar River

North Bentinck Arm

Bella Coola ●

Hagen

20

Dean Channel

King Island

Thorwald Creek

Thorwald Creek

Clayton Falls Creek

Tastsquan Creek

Thorsen Creek

Snootli Creek

Nooliknonnic Creek

Burke Channel

▲ Mt Fougner

Larso Bay

▲ Big Snow Mtn

Mt S

▲ Bentinck Spire

South Bentinck Arm

Kwatna Inlet

Kwatna River

Smitley River

No

Quatlena River

Taleom